DWIGHT D. EISENHOWER
Soldier and President

DWIGHT D. EISENHOWER
Soldier and President

Jeff C. Young

MORGAN
REYNOLDS
Publishers, Inc.

620 South Elm Street, Suite 223
Greensboro, North Carolina   27406
http://www.morganreynolds.com

DWIGHT D. EISENHOWER: SOLDIER AND PRESIDENT

Library of Congress Cataloging-in-Publication Data

Young, Jeff C., 1948-
  Dwight D. Eisenhower : soldier and president / Jeff C. Young.
    p.cm.
  Includes bibliographic references and index.
  ISBN 1-883846-76-5 (lib. bdg.)
    1. Eisenhower, Dwight D. (Dwight David), 1890-1969--Juvenile literature. 2.
  Presidents--United States--Biography--Juvenile literature. 3. Generals--United
  States--Biography--Juvenile literature. 4. United States. Army--Biography--Juvenile
  literature.

  E836. Y68 2001
  973.921'092--dc21
  [B]

                                                          2001030822

Printed in the United States of America
First Edition

To my history mentors—
Ralph W. Stark
Carl W. Riggs
Dwight W. Hoover

Contents

Dwight D. Eisenhower.
(Courtesy of the Dwight D. Eisenhower Library.)

Chapter One

"Little Ike"

Dwight Eisenhower liked to tell his friends how a mean barnyard goose taught him a lesson that he never forgot. When Dwight was four, he visited his Uncle Luther. He was a curious child and he wanted to explore his uncle's farm. But whenever he tried, an angry gander would chase him away. Its aggressive looks and hissing would send Dwight running into the house, whining and crying.

Uncle Luther decided that something had to be done. He chopped off the handle from an old broom and gave it to Dwight for a weapon. The next time the gander came at him, Dwight chased it away. From then on, the gander kept its distance. Dwight learned that the best way to deal with an enemy was from a position of strength. It was a lesson that he would remember when he served as a five-star general in World War II and as president of the United States.

Dwight David Eisenhower was born in Denison, Texas, on October 14, 1890, to David and Ida

Eisenhower. Two brothers had preceded him, Arthur in 1886 and Edgar in 1889, and four more would follow over the next nine years. When David met Ida Stover they were both students at Lane University in Lecompton, Kansas. David was shy and seldom smiled. Ida was outgoing, chatty, and almost always grinning. They seemed to be two very different people, but they married about a year after they first met. They settled in Hope, Kansas, where David opened a general store, but a crooked business partner and poor economic conditions forced him to declare bankruptcy two years later. David had to leave his family behind while he went to Denison, Texas, to look for work.

When Dwight was born, David was making ten dollars a week as a railroad worker. Although his family never had much money, Dwight never felt that they poor. "If we were poor, we were unaware of it," Eisenhower wrote. "We were always well fed, adequately clothed and housed."

Before Dwight's first birthday, the family moved from Denison to Abilene, Kansas, where his father became an engineer at the Belle Springs Creamery. "Engineer" was a high sounding title for a low paying job. The new job paid even less than working for the railroad. David's main duty was to keep the machinery running.

When he enrolled in Abilene's Lincoln School in 1896, Dwight's nickname was "Little Ike." His older brother Edgar, was "Big Ike." Soon, Dwight's friends and classmates began calling him Ike. The nickname

The Eisenhowers' home in 1895.
(Courtesy of the Dwight D. Eisenhower Library.)

stuck and Dwight David Eisenhower would always be known as Ike.

Blond haired, blue-eyed Ike was energetic and rough. He was not a bully, but he never backed down from a fight. One way to always get him to fight was to tease him about his hand-me-down clothes.

About a year after Ike started school, David moved the family into a house on a three-acre lot. The new house had an attic, a basement, and both a winter and summer kitchen. Compared to the cramped houses they had lived in before, the new home was huge to Ike. There was also a barn and an orchard on the property.

A bigger house also meant increased household

chores for Ike and his brothers. There were cows, chickens, and pigs to feed. There were crops to look after. The Eisenhowers were now able to grow their own food and sell what they had left over.

Instead of an allowance, each of the Eisenhower boys were given a plot of land to raise crops to sell. Sweet corn and cucumbers were Ike's cash crops. He used the money he made to buy clothes, a rifle, and football equipment.

Even though school and household chores took up most of the day, Ike and his brothers still found time to play. Sometimes, their curiosity and spirit of adventure would get them into trouble at home.

When a flood hit Abilene, Ike and one of his brothers decided to go exploring. They used a broken piece of a wooden sidewalk as a makeshift raft. While merrily floating down the flooded streets, they failed to notice that they were heading straight for the swollen waters of the raging river.

Fortunately, a worried neighbor made them turn back, probably saving the boys from drowning. When the boys arrived home soaking wet, their father disciplined them with a hickory switch.

Although Ike usually got along with his brothers, sometimes brotherly arguments turned into fights. Most of Ike's fights were with Edgar. No matter how many times Edgar beat him, Ike would challenge him to another fight. Their mother would leave them alone, even when Edgar pinned Ike and battered his head on the

The Eisenhowers in 1902: David, Milton, Ida in the front row; Dwight, Edgar, Earl, Arthur, Roy in the back row. *(Courtesy of the Dwight. D. Eisenhower Library.)*

wooden floor. "You can't keep healthy boys from scrapping," Ida said. "And it isn't any good to interfere too much."

In the Eisenhower home, physical punishment was usually left to the father; lecturing was done by the mother. Ike's most memorable lecture from his mother occurred when he was ten. His parents had told him he was too young to go trick-or-treating with his two older brothers. He pleaded and begged, but they still said no. After his brothers left, Ike became enraged. He stormed out of the house and began beating on the trunk of an apple tree until his fists were bloody and bruised.

The next thing he knew, his father was shaking him by the shoulders. Ike's punishment was swift and sure.

"My father legislated the matter with the traditional hickory switch and sent me off to bed," Ike wrote.

About an hour later, Ike's mother came to his room. Ike was sobbing into his pillow. He was mad that he could not join his older brothers. For a long time, his mother said nothing. Then, she began telling Ike about learning to control his temper. She made her point by quoting the Bible: "He that conquerth his own soul is greater than he who taketh a city."

Ida told Ike that little was to be gained from hating. She also reminded him that the person one hated was probably unaware of it. While applying salve and bandages to her son's swollen fists, she reminded him that he had only hurt himself by his violent display of anger and frustration.

After admitting that he was wrong, Ike calmed down enough to go to sleep. He would later write that this talk with his mother was one of the most valuable moments of his life. Ike would think about his mother's advice at times when he would struggle to keep his explosive temper under control.

Even after he learned to control his temper better, young Ike still had a stubborn streak. When he was a freshman in high school, he fell down and skinned his knee. His knee ached, but he was more worried about his ripped pants.

Two days after the mishap, his knee was still aching, and his left foot was swollen and had turned black. Ida called a doctor. The doctor examined Ike's knee and

The 1909 Abilene High School baseball team. Dwight is fourth from the left on the front row. *(Courtesy of the Dwight D. Eisenhower Library.)*

foot and diagnosed blood poisoning. The doctor spoke privately with Ike's parents. He grimly told them that the leg might have to be amputated. He would know for sure the next day.

Ike was unable to sleep that night. Pain and dread kept him awake. In the morning, Ike could see that the swelling and discoloration had gotten even worse. The doctor told Ike that cutting off part of the leg would save the rest of it. It would also save Ike's life.

Ike stubbornly told the doctor that he would rather die than lose any part of his leg. If he were unable to run, jump, or play sports, life would be unbearable. Ike made his brother Edgar promise him that he would keep the doctor from their bedroom.

Edgar stood guard outside of the bedroom door for two days. Even when his brother was screaming in pain, Edgar did not waver. The doctor pleaded with Ike's parents to let him amputate, but Edgar prevailed. Eventually, the swelling receded. In about three weeks, Ike was up and walking around again. The doctor called it a miracle. David and Ida thought it was an answered prayer. The following autumn, Dwight returned to school to repeat his freshman year.

Ike returned to high school wanting to make up for lost time. He resumed playing football and baseball. In those days, the school did not provide sports equipment. Ike and his classmates founded the Abilene High School Athletic Association. The association's dues of twenty-five cents a month helped to pay for footballs, pads, and other equipment. During his senior year, Ike served as the association's president.

Math and history were Ike's favorite subjects. He also showed an avid interest in military history, but not the details. He only wanted to know the final result.

Ike's math skills were whetted by his love for poker. An older friend named Bob Davis had taught him the game. Although illiterate, Davis was a self-sufficient outdoorsman. Ike's father worked so often he never had much time for his sons, so Davis became sort of a substitute father and mentor. He taught Ike how to hunt, trap, boat, and fish. Davis also taught Ike how to determine the odds of drawing a better card in a hand of poker. The two played for matches.

Years later, Ike would recall, "So thoroughly did Bob drill me on percentages that I continued to play poker until I was thirty-eight or forty and I was never able to play the game carelessly or wide open. I adhered strictly to percentages. Since most tyros and many vets know nothing about probabilities, it was not remarkable that I should be a regular winner."

Before he graduated from high school, Ike also tried his hand at acting. Ike's senior class performed a take-off on Shakespeare's *The Merchant of Venice*. Ike hammed it up by playing the comical role of Lancelot Gobbo. He put red powder in his hair and blacked out two front teeth with gum. The Abilene newspaper praised Ike's performance, writing that Ike "was the best amateur humorous character seen on the Abilene stage in this generation and gave an impression that many professional (actors) fail to reach."

Ike and Edgar both graduated from Abilene High School on May 23, 1909. They both wanted to go to college, but knew they would have to pay for it themselves. Their family could not afford to send either one of them off to school.

The brothers made a deal. Edgar would go to the University of Michigan while Ike worked. If necessary, Edgar would later drop out of school so Ike could go. It would take a long time, but both of them would eventually get a college education.

Ike went to work in the creamery with his father. Ike already knew the job, since he had worked there part time since his early teens. As well as working twelve hours a day, six days a week, Ike played baseball for Abilene's semipro team. He also worked at a farm and at a factory that made steel grain bins. "I changed from one job to another, depending on the prospects for an extra dime an hour or an extra dollar a day," Eisenhower recalled. Thanks to his brother's help, Edgar started college in the fall of 1909.

If it were not for a friend, Ike might have stayed at the creamery for a long time. Everett Hazlett had attended military school and had applied to the U.S. Naval Academy at Annapolis, Maryland, but he had failed the math portion of the entrance exam. When Everett got a reappointment to the academy, he asked Ike to take the entrance exam with him.

Ike saw an appointment to a military academy as an opportunity to start college ahead of schedule. It was also a chance at a free education. Ike and Everett began studying together three or four hours a day. Ike also returned to high school to take refresher courses in some of his weaker subjects.

Ike needed a recommendation from a member of Congress before he could take the entrance exam. Many of Abilene's most prominent citizens wrote letters of support on Ike's behalf to Kansas Senator Joseph L. Bristow. Bristow recommended Ike. In the summer of 1910, Ike took the entrance exams for both the Naval Academy and the U. S. Military Academy at West Point, New York.

Before Ike even knew his test results, he received news that he was too old to enter the Naval Academy, where a freshman could not be a day over twenty. Ike would be nearly twenty-one when the next class entered. It seemed that Ike's dream of a free college education was shattered.

It was a hollow victory when Ike read his test results. He had placed first among candidates from his state for Annapolis and second for West Point. His only hope was a slim chance of going to West Point as an alternate.

Sometimes when one door of opportunity closes, another opens. That's what happened to Ike. The top-ranked candidate for West Point failed his physical. In the spring of 1911, Senator Bristow appointed Dwight Eisenhower for admission to the U.S. Military Academy in West Point, New York.

In his understated manner, Ike wrote, "This was a good day in my life."

Chapter Two

West Point

On a sunny June morning in 1911, Ike said goodbye to his tearful mother and proud father. Leaving Abilene with one suitcase and five dollars in his wallet, Ike boarded a train for New York. Before reaching West Point, Ike stopped off at Ann Arbor, Michigan, to visit Edgar at the university.

Even though Edgar was taking his end of the year exams, the brothers found time to have some fun. One evening they went canoeing down the Huron River with two coeds. Ike remembered the canoe trip as, "the most romantic evening I had ever known." The time he enjoyed with the coeds gave Ike some misgivings as he traveled on to the all-male military academy.

Ike's doubts continued to grow when he arrived at West Point. Cadets barked orders in his face as soon as he got off the train.

"Get your shoulders back! Suck in that stomach! Drag in your chin! Hurry up! Hurry up!" Everything was done in double time. No matter how much he hustled, Ike could not move fast enough to suit the upperclassmen.

The constant orders and shouts of disapproval were known as hazing. Plebes (first year students) were addressed as "Mr. Dumbjohn" or "Mr. Dumbgard." There was physical harassment as well. Plebes were ordered to pick ants out of an anthill, one at a time, and they were also routinely ordered to do push-ups and other hard exercises.

Because he was almost as old as most of the cadets bossing him around, Ike took the hazing in good humor. The way he saw it, he was getting paid to get a college education. He was determined the upperclassmen would not run him off.

Not all of Ike's classmates were able to endure the persistent abuse. Ike's first roommate was a sensitive seventeen-year-old boy who cried every night. He left the academy before the end of the first semester.

Because he saw little or no purpose in hazing, Ike did not participate when he became an upperclassman. The only time he hazed another cadet, Ike felt badly about it.

A plebe was double-timing across campus while carrying out an order, not watching where he was going. He collided with Ike and then fell to the ground. Ike pretended to be mad and began addressing the fallen cadet in a sarcastic manner. "Mr. Dumbgard what is your P.C.S. [previous condition of servitude]?" Ike demanded. "You look like a barber," Ike scoffed.

"I was a barber, sir," the cadet humbly replied.

Ike was so embarrassed, his face turned red. After returning to his living quarters, Ike told his roommate: "I'm never going to crawl [haze] another plebe as long as I live. I've done something that was stupid and unforgivable. I managed to make a man ashamed of what he did to earn a living."

At the academy, Ike worked harder at athletics than academics. He was still passionate about baseball and football. But when he tried out for the academy's teams he found himself competing against bigger and more talented athletes.

Ike was strong and muscular, but he only weighed 152 pounds. Although he was too light for football, he was determined to try in the fall. In baseball, he was a good fielder, but the coach did not like his hitting style. In high school, Ike had learned to be a "chop" hitter, one who hit the ball at selected locations. The academy coach told him he would have to change his style. "Practice hitting my way for a year, and you'll be on my squad next spring," the coach said.

Ike worked hard all summer getting ready for football. He started the season with high hopes. A preseason preview in the *New York Times* called Ike, "one of the most promising backs in Eastern football."

But his chances for football glory came to an end. In

a game against Tufts College, Ike twisted his knee. He was carried off the field. Although his knee was badly swollen, Ike felt little pain. He was hospitalized for three days, and afterwards, he quickly resumed his normal activities.

A few days after being released, Ike was practicing a horse riding drill with some other cadets. Ike re-injured his knee after leaping from a galloping horse. The cartilage and tendons were badly torn. Ike's leg was put in a plaster cast. This time, there was intense pain. Ike had trouble sleeping. While awake, he was constantly depressed and irritable.

Ike was even more gloomy after the cast was removed. The doctors told him he would never play football again. Ike thought about leaving West Point, but some friends talked him out of it. Still, he was so depressed he had little interest in his studies or anything else. "Life seemed to have little meaning," Ike would recall. "A need to excel was almost gone."

After his freshmen year, Ike stood fifty-seventh in his class of 212. Following the knee injury, he dropped to eighty-first out of 177. Ike also became more rebellious. He started smoking and piling up demerits for bad behavior. Cadets could smoke pipes and cigars, but cigarettes were strictly forbidden. Ike flaunted the rule by taking up cigarettes.

Since cigarettes were unavailable on campus, Ike rolled his own. He smoked openly and was careless about getting caught. His usual punishment was confinement to living quarters or marching for a long time while shouldering a rifle. Ike would accept the punishment and demerits without complaining.

Ike also racked up additional demerits for refusing to keep his room tidy and being habitually late for formations or guard duty. One time, Ike and another plebe made an upperclassman named Corporal Adler look silly by obeying his orders to the letter.

Adler had found the cadets guilty of "a minor infraction." He ordered Ike and the other plebe to report to his room in "full-dress coats," or complete uniform. They took the order literally and reported wearing their full-dress coats—and nothing else.

Adler was furious. Some upperclassmen heard his roar of disapproval and rushed to his room to see what was going on. Some of them thought it was hilarious. Others thought it was affront to their dignity and rank.

Ike and his friend paid for their prank by having to stand at attention for a long time and listen to a lengthy lecture about their bad behavior. When the punishment was over, the sweat-stained outlines of their backs and shoulders could be seen on the barracks wall.

On another occasion, Ike's total disregard of the academy's rules earned him a demotion. At a cadet dance, Ike asked a professor's daughter to dance. The customary dances at these events were sedate two-step polkas and waltzes. Those dances were too confining for Ike and his partner.

"This girl and I liked to whirl; just whirling around

After a hard week of study and drills, Ike Eisenhower enjoyed social dances at West Point. *(Courtesy of the Dwight D. Eisenhower Library.)*

the room as rapidly as we could," Ike recalled. "I suppose the exercise probably showed a little more of the girl's ankles, possibly reaching even to her knees, than the sharp-eye authorities thought was seemly. I was warned not to dance that way any more."

A few months later, Ike was at another dance. His mind was far from dancing, however, because he was in the middle of one of his marathon poker games. He had just dropped by the dance for some free refreshments. While he was there, he chanced to see his dance partner, the professor's daughter. Soon, they were once again whirling their way across the dance floor.

Ike was summoned to see the academy's Commandant. He was reprimanded for improper dancing and for ignoring a previous warning. Ike was demoted from sergeant to private.

When Ike wanted to get serious, he was a good student. In a typical class at West Point, instructors would ask questions and cadets would respond with memorized answers. Ike had a retentive mind and was good at recalling the answers. He stayed in the top half of his class without studying very hard and did not let academics interfere with his card playing or athletics.

In a calculus class, Ike surprised his instructor by offering a shorter and simpler solution to a long, complicated problem. Ike and his eleven classmates had been ordered to memorize a long and involved solution to a problem. Ike had failed to memorize the approved solution, reasoning that there was a one-to-eleven chance he would be called on. "Because I was a lazy student, with considerable faith in my luck, I decided there was little use in trying to understand the solution," he said later.

When the instructor called on him, Ike approached the blackboard without "the foggiest notion of how to begin." Luckily, Ike did remember the answer the instructor had given. He began by writing it in the corner of the blackboard. It took Ike nearly an hour to find a solution. Ike checked his work and then confidently returned to his desk.

After Ike had worked out the problem, the instructor accused him of trickery. He declared that Ike had merely written down a bunch of meaningless steps and figures to fit the answer. Ike was not about to be called a cheat.

Ike prepared to rebut the accusation, but before he could speak, another instructor interupted him. A senior officer in the mathematics department had walked in for a surprise inspection. The senior officer asked Ike to repeat his explanation.

Ike went through the problem again. The senior officer said that Ike's solution was superior to the one the academy had been using, and he ordered that Ike's solution replace it.

Once Ike got over the disappointment and depression of his knee injury, he immersed himself in other activities. He remained connected to the football team by becoming a cheerleader. That position gave him his first experience in public speaking. The night before a big game, Ike would address the entire corps of cadets and urge them to back the team.

Ike's enthusiasm and knowledge of football also got him the job of junior varsity coach. He compiled a winning record and several of his players went on to have successful varsity careers. As a coach, he showed some of the traits that would later make him an outstanding military and political leader: organizational ability, competitiveness, a strong work ethic, and the ability to get the most out of the material he was given.

A few weeks before graduation, it looked as if Ike would be denied a commission as an officer in the army. The academy's chief medical officer was concerned about Ike's knee. The doctor told Ike he was reluctant to recommend him for a commission. Ike surprised the doctor by telling him he was not very concerned. He had been reading up on Argentina, he said. He had thought about settling there if the army refused him. Even if he lost a commission, he would still have a free college degree. The army could not take that away from him.

As a sort of counter-proposal, the doctor offered Ike a less physically demanding commission in the cost artillery. There would be little or no chance of Ike re-injuring his knee at that post.

Ike turned it down. The doctor made him another offer. If Ike would apply for service in the infantry, the doctor would approve him for a commission. Ike agreed, mainly because he felt he lacked anything better to do.

When he graduated in 1915, academically Ike was ranked sixty-one in a class of 164. His poor discipline record lowered his class standing to 125 in discipline because of his 211 demerits. The school yearbook called Ike "as big as life and twice as natural." Ike was well liked by his fellow cadets, but some members of the faculty had mixed feelings about his commitment to the army.

One tactical officer said Ike "would thoroughly enjoy his army life, giving both to duty and recreation their fair values, [but] we did not see in him a man who would throw himself into his job so completely that nothing else would be better." Another officer's assessment was more accurate. He wrote that Ike "was born to command."

After being commissioned, Ike requested the Philippines as his first tour of duty. He was the only member of his class to seek that assignment. Ike saw the army as a chance for a small town Kansas boy to see the world. If he could not go to Argentina, then the Philippines would be okay. Ike was certain that was where he was going. He spent all his clothing allowance on tropical uniforms made of khaki and white linen.

Ike used his graduation leave to return to Abilene and await his orders. In mid-September of 1915, they arrived. Instead of the Philippines, Ike would be stationed stateside at the 19th Infantry Regiment at Fort Sam Houston near San Antonio, Texas.

Chapter Three

Army Man

Despite his disappointment at not being sent overseas, Ike discovered that Fort Sam Houston was a pleasant place to be stationed. The duties assigned to a young second lieutenant were not very taxing. Most officers finished their daily duties and work assignments before noon and spent the rest of the day hunting and horseback riding. After dinner, there were dances, bachelor parties, and poker games.

Along with his poker winnings, Ike supplemented his $141.67 a month salary by coaching football at the local military academy. At first, Ike turned the coaching job down, but his commanding officer changed his mind by telling him, "It would please me and it would be good for the Army if you would accept this offer." Ike realized that anything that was good for the army was also good for his career.

One sunny afternoon in October, Ike was serving as Officer of the Day. After walking out of his residence at the bachelor officer quarters, he heard someone calling his name. A wife of a major asked Ike to meet some of her friends. "Sorry," Ike replied. "I'm on guard and I have to start an inspection trip." The major's wife pretended to be upset. She teased Ike by calling him "the woman-hater of the post." Then she told Ike, "We didn't ask you to come over to stay. Just come over here and meet these friends of mine."

Her friends were a family named Doud. They were from Denver but spent their winters in San Antonio. Ike was immediately attracted to their eighteen-year-old daughter, Mamie. "The one who attracted my eye instantly was a vivacious and attractive girl, smaller than average, saucy in look about her face and in her whole attitude," Ike recalled. "I was intrigued by her appearance."

Ike impulsively asked Mamie to accompany him on his rounds about the base. To his delight, she said yes. Soon, Ike was calling her several times a day. On Valentine's Day, he gave her his West Point class ring. They were married in Denver on July 1, 1916.

The newlyweds did not have much of a honeymoon. Ike had been granted only a ten-day furlough for his wedding, and the ceremony was arranged on such short notice that his parents could not attend. Before returning to San Antonio, Ike and Mamie stopped in Abilene so David and Ida could meet their daughter-in-law.

Back at Fort Sam Houston, Ike and Mamie loved entertaining friends. Their three-room apartment soon became one of the base's social centers and came to be known as "Club Eisenhower."

The parties came to an abrupt end when the United States entered World War I in April of 1917. Ike was promoted to a Captain and reassigned to Fort Ogelthorpe, Georgia. Mamie stayed at Fort Sam Houston while Ike trained young recruits for combat.

The years of World War I were very difficult for Ike. He yearned to be fighting in Europe with the other infantry officers and made repeated requests for over-seas duty. He was turned down every time. His assignment also kept him separated from Mamie when their first child, Doud Dwight, was born on September 24, 1917.

In mid-December, Ike was given orders to report to Fort Leavenworth, Kansas. Before reporting, the army allowed Ike to return to Fort Sam Houston to visit his wife and infant son, whom they had nicknamed "Icky."

At Leavenworth, Ike first showed his flair for leadership. One of his superiors wrote: "Our new Captain, Eisenhower by name, is, I believe, one of the most efficient and best Army officers in the country. He has given us wonderful bayonet drills. He gets the fellows' imaginations worked up and hollers and yells and makes us shout and stomp until we go tearing into the air as if we mean business."

Ike was still determined to experience combat. He enrolled in the army's first tank school and was assigned to Camp Meade, Maryland, in February of 1918.

Ike was thrilled with this new opportunity. A tank battalion was scheduled to arrive in France in the spring, and he hoped he would finally experience combat.

Anticipation turned to disappointment when Ike received his next set of orders. His superiors had such high praise for his organizational ability that they decided to keep Ike stateside. He was dispatched to Camp Colt in Gettysburg, Pennsylvania.

If it had been peacetime, Ike would have really liked his new duty post. He was promoted to major and at the age of twenty-seven was commanding thousands of men. He was able to rent a house and reunite with Mamie and Icky.

The tank was a new weapon; so new, the army did not have any for Ike and his men to use for training. They simulated firing from a tank by mounting machine guns on flatbed trucks.

By mid-July, Ike had 10,000 enlisted men and 600 officers under his command. He worked tirelessly to turn a Civil War battlefield into an army camp. Ike's hard work and long hours did not go unnoticed. On his twenty-eighth birthday, he was promoted to lieutenant colonel.

Along with the promotion, Ike received another unexpected birthday gift: He got his orders to go overseas. He was ordered to leave for France on November 18, 1918, to command an armored unit. The United States and its allies had planned a massive armored attack for the spring of 1919.

Ike put Mamie and Icky on a train to Denver. He went to New York to make sure his men were ready to ship out. Then, one week before his scheduled departure, World War I suddenly ended. On November 11, 1918, Germany signed an armistice, ending the war.

Ike was profoundly depressed. He feared that he would spend the rest of his life explaining why he missed combat in World War I.

With the war's end, the army began demobilizing. Thousands of soldiers were discharged and wartime promotions were rescinded. Ike was demoted from lieutenant colonel to captain. A decrease in rank also meant a decrease in pay. Ike considered leaving the army. In peacetime, it would probably take Ike another fifteen years to again become a lieutenant colonel. But Ike enjoyed army life because it offered travel, education, friendships, and affordable housing. He turned down better paying civilian jobs.

In the summer of 1919, Ike travelled in a convoy of military vehicles on a cross-country trip from Washington, D.C. to San Francisco, California. The purpose of the trip was to test army vehicles and to publicize the need for better roads. The nation's road system was so bad that some days the convoy only averaged about five miles per hour.

The trip was like a paid vacation. Ike got to see the country while traveling at a leisurely pace. Along the way, the soldiers enjoyed camping, hunting, fishing, and poker games.

Ike's next assignment sent him to Camp Meade, Maryland, to train tank crews. It was here that Ike first met George S. Patton, who would become a renowned tank commander in World War II. Ike and Patton soon became good friends. They spent hours studying and discussing military history. The young officers shared a firm belief that the tank was the weapon of the future.

Ike and Patton wrote articles in military journals arguing that tanks of the future would need to be bigger, faster, and more heavily armored than the ones used in World War I. History would show they were right, but the U.S. army believed that future wars would be won by foot soldiers and not by machines.

Ike's duty at Camp Meade left time for play. Ike and Mamie hosted parties, and "Club Eisenhower" was once again the social center of the army base. To help with the housework and entertaining, the Eisenhowers hired a maid. This decision resulted in tragic consequences.

Ike and Mamie were unaware that the young girl they hired had recently recovered from scarlet fever. Apparently, she passed the disease on to Icky, who became ill. A specialist from Johns Hopkins University in Baltimore was brought in, but there was nothing he could do. There was no cure for the disease. The specialist could only tell Ike and Mamie to pray. Icky was quarantined and his father could not even enter the hospital room.

Icky fought the disease for about two weeks before dying on January 2, 1920. Ike and Mamie blamed themselves for his death. Ike wrote that Icky's death "was the greatest disappointment and disaster in my life."

A new assignment and environment ultimately brought Ike and Mamie out of their profound grief. In January of 1922, Ike was asigned to serve in the Canal Zone in Panama.

He served under General Fox Conner. Conner became much more than Ike's commanding officer. He became a mentor and role model who would teach Ike more military history than he had learned at West Point.

Conner had first met Ike while visiting Patton at Camp Meade. Conner knew about Ike and Patton's work with tanks, and he asked them to share their knowledge and expertise. They spent an afternoon showing Conner around Camp Meade, expaining their vision of the tank as the weapon of the future. At the end of the visit, Conner encouraged the young officers to continue their work.

Conner had Ike read books on military history and strategy. The assigned readings included the memoirs of Civil War generals and a very difficult book by Karl von Clausewitz entitled *On War*. Conner would ask Ike probing questions about what he read and decisions made by military leaders. What if they had acted differently? What were their alternatives?

Conner also got Ike to think about future world events. Conner predicted that there would be another world war in twenty years or less. He advised Ike to seek an appointment under General George C. Marshall because he believed Marshall would be one of America's major military leaders in the next world war.

Ike called his three years in Panama "a sort of graduate school in military affairs." He would remember Conner as "the one figure to whom I owe incalculable debt."

Another event that made Ike's tenure in Panama a pleasant time was the birth of his second son, John Sheldon Doud Eisenhower, on August 3, 1923. John's birth helped to ease Ike and Mamie's sorrow over Icky's death.

In 1925, Conner used his influence to get Ike assigned to the Command and General Staff School at Fort Leavenworth, Kansas. Admission to the school was regarded as both a great honor and a grueling challenge. Only 275 of the army's best and brightest officers were admitted. Ike wrote Conner and expressed doubts about how he would do in such a high pressure, competitive environment. Conner wrote Ike back and assured him he had nothing to worry about.

The one-year course mostly consisted of problem solving in war games and imaginary battles. Students were told their army had to attack or defend a position. They would have to make detailed decisions on the movement of troops and supply services. Basically, the students learned how to wage war without firing a shot.

Ike excelled at mastering details and putting ideas into action. He showed his classmates and instructors he could lead while still being a team player. Ike vindicated Conner's confidence by graduating first in his class.

Ike's next post was Washington, D.C., where he wrote a history of the U.S. Army in France in World War I. That assignment was followed with an appointment to the Army War College from 1928 to 1929.

After graduating from the War College, the army gave Ike the choice to go either to Washington, D.C., or to Paris. Ike preferred Washington, but Mamie convinced him to go to Paris. They stayed for fifteen months and opened a European version of "Club Eisenhower."

Upon returning from Paris, Ike worked in Washington for the Assistant Secretary of War. He stayed there until 1932. Then he began one of the most exciting and frustrating periods of his military career. He became the assistant to Army Chief of Staff Douglas MacArthur.

Colorful, brilliant, and egotistical, General MacArthur had an unabashed ambition to become president of the United States. The relationship between Ike and MacArthur was complex. They had their disagreements, and MacArthur was accused of undermining Ike's chances of promotion. The fact is both men benefited from their working relationship. Ike said he was "deeply grateful for the administrative experience he had gained under General MacArthur." He acknowledged that working for MacArthur prepared him for his supreme commander role in World War II.

MacArthur recognized Ike's talents and leadership ability. In an evaluation, MacArthur praised Ike: "This is the best officer in the Army. When the next war comes, he should go right to the top."

General Douglas MacArthur (center) stands among troops with Colonel Dwight D. Eisenhower (right, with his hand at his mouth) during the Bonus March on Washington, D. C. in 1932. When World War I veterans demanded early payment of their service bonuses, President Hoover ordered MacArthur to break up the protest. *(Courtesy of the Library of Congress.)*

In 1935, MacArthur's tenure as Chief of Staff ended. Ike was hoping for a new assignment, but MacArthur was adamant about keeping Ike on his staff. Ike went with his boss to the Philippines.

The United States had acquired the Philippines from Spain in 1898. In 1935, the 7,000-island nation became a commonwealth possession of the U.S. It was scheduled to become an independent country in 1946. MacArthur and Ike's job was to create and train an army of native Filipinos so that the new country could provide for its own protection.

Ike and MacArthur faced a near impossible task. Both the U.S. Congress and the Philippine Legislature neglected to appropriate sufficient funds for an adequate army.

General MacArthur made Ike's job even more difficult by refusing to meet with Philippine President Manuel Quezon. Ike wrote: "He [MacArthur] apparently thinks it would not be in keeping with his rank and position to do so."

Ike did receive some compensation for living and working in a remote, tropical country. He learned to fly and spent many happy hours piloting a plane. He got extra pay and enjoyed luxurious, air conditioned living quarters. Mamie and John were able to live with him, although Mamie complained about the tropical climate.

Overall, Ike felt that the negatives of his years in the Philippines outweighed the positives. He wanted to be stationed elsewhere, but MacArthur wanted him to stay.

GERMAN LEGIONS MARCH INTO REMILITARIZED RHINE-
LAND MARCH 7, 1936

HITLER BECOMES DICTATOR
JANUARY 30, 1933

GERMANS GRAB SUDETENLAND
OCTOBER 11, 1938

HITLER FORCES BOHEMIA, MORAVIA
AND SLOVAKIA TO SURRENDER TO
NAZIS, MARCH 15, 1939

AS A RESULT OF PLEBISCITE JANUARY 14, 1935, REICH
TAKES OVER SAAR MARCH 1, 1935

HITLER SEIZES AUSTRIA
MARCH 12, 1938

The Nazi army began marching on neighboring countries shortly after Hitler became
dictator.

Then, in September of 1939, Germany invaded Poland. England and France quickly declared war on Germany. Ike appealed to the War Department for an immediate transfer. Another world war seemed inevitable,
and Ike got his wish. He was needed back in the United
States to help prepare the army. In December of 1939,
Ike, Mamie, and John left the Philippines, and
MacArthur, behind.

During the voyage, Ike and John had a heart-to-heart
talk. John was seventeen and he wanted to emulate his
father by going to West Point and becoming a career
army officer. Ike had never pushed John in that direction. He was delighted that his son was thinking about
it, but Ike candidly told John what he could expect from

a career in a peacetime army. He told John that in other professions such as medicine, law, or business, one could go as far as one's talents, ambitions, and character could take one. In the army, no matter how good one was, or how well one performed, the rules of seniority governed promotions. Ike's career was a perfect example. Over twenty-nine years he had consistently received excellent evaluations, had graduated first in his class at Command and General Staff School, but those achievements and accolades had done little to advance his career. He was still a captain.

Members of West Point's class of 1915 would not even be eligible for promotion to colonel until 1950. By then, Ike would be sixty and close to mandatory retirement. Ike told his son, his own chances of becoming a general "were nil."

On the positive side, the work was interesting. There was travel and the satisfaction of working with dedicated and talented men serving their country. Finally, John felt the pluses outweighed the negatives. He pleased his father by enrolling in West Point.

After four years in the Philippines, Ike was back to the land that he loved. In spite of the troubling events in Europe, Ike hoped that he and John would spend their careers in a peacetime army.

Chapter Four

Supreme Commander

Ike's new assignment at Fort Lewis, Washington, was training troops to make them combat ready. He felt revitalized after spending four years in the Philippines. In a letter to his old West Point classmate General Omar Bradley, Ike wrote: "I'm having the time of my life. Like everything else in the Army, we're up to our neck in work and problems, big and little. But this work is fun . . . I could not conceive of a better job."

New responsibilities also gave Ike a new rank. In March of 1941, he finally became a colonel. In June, he returned to Fort Sam Houston to serve as General Walter Krueger's Chief of Staff. Ike and Mamie were able to celebrate their twenty-fifth wedding anniversary at the base where they first met.

During August and September of 1941, the U.S. Army held their largest maneuvers prior to entering World War II. The war games pitted General Krueger and Ike's 240,000-man Second Army against General Ben Lear's 180,000-man Third Army.

Using strategy Ike had helped to plan, the Second Army outflanked the Lear's Third Army and forced them to retreat. Ike received most of the credit for the victory, but he said it should go to General Krueger. The *New York Times* reported, "Had it been a real war, Lear's force would have been annihilated."

The army took notice of Ike's outstanding performance. Acting upon the recommendation of General Krueger, Ike was promoted to brigadier general ahead of 366 officers with more seniority.

Sunday morning, December 7, 1941, started off as another quiet day at Fort Sam Houston. Mamie wanted Ike to stay at home, but he insisted on going into his office to catch up on some paper work. Around noon, he went home for a nap. Ike had been asleep for about an hour when he received a phone call informing him that the Japanese had bombed Pearl Harbor, Hawaii.

For the next five days, Ike literally worked around the clock. The nonstop pace continued until he received a call from the War Department, ordering him to immediately report to Army Chief of Staff, General George C. Marshall. Ike assumed his visit to Washington, D.C. would be a short He only packed one bag and told Mamie he would be home soon.

General George C. Marshall was an official and distant man. When Ike reported to him on December 14, 1941, Marshall asked him to formulate a plan to help General MacArthur repel a Japanese invasion of the Philippines. Ike asked Marshall to give him a few hours.

The assessment Ike gave was blunt and candid. In his opinion, the Philippines were indefensible. They would fall to the Japanese, but the U.S. could not abandon them. The best plan was to establish a base of operations in Australia and to begin preparing a counterattack. In the meantime, the U.S. should supply General MacArthur and his troops all the planes, pilots, arms, and other materials they could spare.

General Marshall was impressed by Ike's candor and understanding of military realities. He appreciated that the bad news had been delivered in a forthright manner. He told Ike that he agreed with him. As Fox Conner and General MacArthur had done before, General Marshall became Ike's mentor and benefactor.

General Marshall grew to respect and rely on Ike because they thought alike. Marshall wanted junior officers around him who were calm, confident, and offensive-minded in waging war. He wanted officers with a positive outlook and a dedication to duty. Ike learned how to think like General Marshall. He soon could learn to anticipate an order and get it done before it had been given. General Marshall's reliance on Ike and overall high opinion of him is reflected in his quick ascension through the ranks. In the short span of five months, Ike received three major promotions.

In February 1942, Ike was promoted to the rank of major (two star) general and named chief of the general staff's operation division. This gave him immense power as the army prepared forces to be sent to Europe.

Ike loved his work for Marshall. But what he wanted more than anything was to lead the troops in Europe. He still resented not being allowed to serve in World War I. He feared that his lack of combat experience in that war would undermine his chances for an active command. He faced the prospect of spending the entire war helping Marshall with the administrative work in Washington.

While serving with Marshall, Ike developed a strategy for the war in Europe. "Operation Roundup" called for the accumulation of massive troops and supplies in Europe. Then, instead of making attacks on the "edges" of the land occupied by Germany, such as those in North Africa as the British were proposing, Ike advocated a massive attack against the German armies in France. The German western push had stopped in France as they turned their attention to fighting the Russians in the east. To Ike, and Marshall, it seemed to be a good time to attack with full force. They wanted to attack in the spring of 1943.

Ike was sent to England to try to convince the British of his plan. The British, however, insisted that they could not be ready for a huge attack in such a short time. Prime Minister Churchill and Field Marshal Bernard L. Montgomery wanted to build up the forces for a later attack across the English Channel. In the meantime, they suggested attacking the German forces in North Africa.

Ike left England without reaching a final decision on

Field Marshall General Montgomery and Winston Churchill talk in an airfield in Britain. *(Courtesy of the Library of Congress.)*

how or when to attack the Germans positioned across the English Channel. He did, however, make an impression on the British leaders, especially Churchill and Lord Mountbatten, a member of the royal family who served as an admiral in the British Navy. Both men suggested to Marshall that Ike be made the top American commander in Europe.

In July of 1942, Ike got a third star on his shoulder when he was promoted to lieutenant general. He was also ordered to return to London to serve as the American commander.

Back in England, Ike worked eighteen and twenty hour days. When he was not working on war plans, he was encouraging harmony among Americans, British, and French soldiers. Although they were wartime allies, the British were weary of American soldiers stationed in and around London. By British standards, American soldiers were overpaid. The British also felt the "Yanks" spent too much time drinking in pubs and wooing British women.

Ike acted quickly to change the attitudes of the American soldiers. He started a program to educate American troops in British customs and history. Ike also organized mandatory bus tours of London so that American soldiers could see the bombed sections of the city. Most importantly, he instilled a sense of military discipline and pride in troops accustomed to working a five-day week. The British noticed these changes and Ike became the most-liked American in London.

Ike was also able to develop his relationships with Britain's important military and political leaders. The most important of these leaders was Prime Minister Winston Churchill. Ike's informal manner appealed to Churchill. Although they would later have disagreements on the conduct of the war, they still maintained a strong mutual respect. They never let their arguments and bickering affect their friendship.

Unfortunately, Ike did not enjoy such a warm relationship with Field Marshal Bernard L. Montgomery. They simply disliked each other and their conversations were always strained. Ike liked to do things by committee and reach a consensus. Montgomery preferred to work alone.

It soon became clear that Ike's dream of an early frontal attack on German troops in France was not going to become a reality. There were not enough supplies and men for it to be a success. In addition, it became clear after he assumed command that the American troops had not been sufficiently trained for such a dangerous operation. It was agreed that the British plan of an attack against the Germans in North Africa would be the Allies' first move. They would destroy Germany's fuel supplies and to capture the tank troops that had terrorized the flat plains.

Under Ike's supreme command a joint force of 400,000 American, British, and French troops invaded Morocco and Algeria in North Africa on November 8, 1942. At first, the fighting went badly for the Allies.

British Field Marshal Bernard Montgomery forced German General Edwin Rommel and his tank corps to retreat from Libya to Tunisia. The Allies hoped to win a quick victory by attacking the rear flank of the retreating troops.

Unfortunately, the strategy failed. The American troops and their commanders were inexperienced. Coordination between the commands was plagued by squabbles between the French and British, poor communication, lack of transport and inadequate intelligence gathering. It was clear that victory would be months away.

Despite the early setbacks in North Africa, Ike received his fourth star on February 11, 1943. The fighting continued. There were several failed attempts to turn the flank of the Germans and Italians. Each time Rommel and the other experienced Axis (the name given to the combined German and Italian troops) leaders were able to slip through the noose.

Then, in May of 1943, the 275,000 Italian and German troops in Tunisia surrendered. North Africa was liberated. Now Ike and the Allied forces could turn their energy and attention to the next phase of the liberation of Europe—the invasion of Sicily and Italy.

Sicily was the gateway to Italy. The mountainous 9,300-square-mile island lay off of Italy's southern coast. In the summer of 1943, it was heavily fortified and occupied by the German Army.

Before the Allied forces could invade Sicily, Ike had

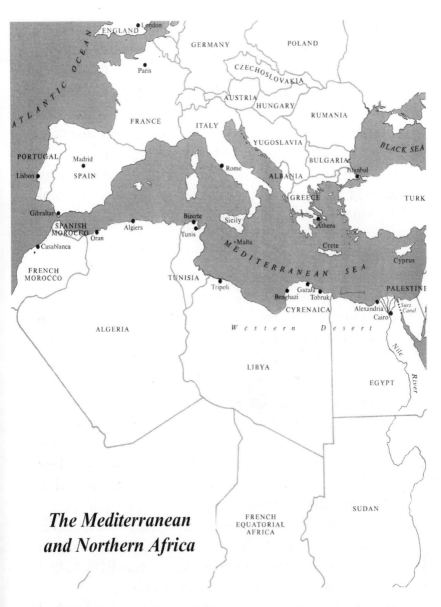

The Mediterranean and Northern Africa

The North Africa campaign stretched from Casablanca in the west to Alexandria and Cairo in the east.

to smooth over relations between President Franklin D. Roosevelt, British Prime Minister Winston Churchill, and the leader of the French Resistance, Charles de Gaulle. After France fell to the Nazis, the armed resistance inside occupied France formed a National Council that proclaimed its loyalty to de Gaulle. President Roosevelt disliked de Gaulle and wanted the Allies to withhold their support of him. Churchill supported de Gaulle because the French leader was so well-liked by his conquered countrymen. Ike had to find a way to please both leaders.

The popularity of de Gaulle in recently liberated Algeria made things even more difficult for Ike. A civil war could break out if the Allies forced de Gaulle out of power or failed to recognize him as the legitimate leader of the French Resistance. If there was turmoil in North Africa, the invasion of Sicily could be doomed to fail. Because the invasion had to be launched from North Africa, chaotic conditions there would leave the rear flank of the invaders vulnerable to attack.

After assuring President Franklin D. Roosevelt that he could "control" de Gaulle, Ike got the president to recognize de Gaulle as the leader of France. Years later, de Gaulle would become president of France while Ike was president of the United States. The two men never became close friends, but they had a healthy mutual respect for each other. De Gaulle respected Ike for his honesty and candor. Ike admired de Gaulle for his political skills and his devotion to France.

On July 10, 1943, Sicily was invaded by a contingent of American, Canadian, British, and French troops, combined with a fleet of 2,500 ships. Within twenty-four hours, several cities in southern Sicily were captured. Thousands of Italian troops soon surrendered, but the outnumbered Germans showed strong resistance.

The invasion was hampered by arguments between American and British field commanders, giving German troops time to retreat and to avoid capture. Still, Sicily was conquered by mid-August, providing the Allied forces a base for launching an attack on the Italian peninsula.

The invasion of Italy began on September 3, 1943. Once again, Italian troops were routed, but the Germans fought furiously. It would take the Allied forces nine months to drive the Germans out of Italy.

In December of 1943, President Franklin D. Roosevelt announced Ike's selection as supreme Allied commander for the invasion of Western Europe. While making the announcement, President Roosevelt lauded Ike's recent accomplishments: "The performances in Africa, Sicily and Italy have been brilliant. He knows by practical and successful experience the way to coordinate air, sea and land power."

This new assignment shifted Ike's focus from Italy. He had a great deal of work to do before the invasion of France could take place. But first he needed a vacation. At the end of December 1943, Ike took his first furlough in two years. Marshall had made repeated requests for Ike to take some time off, but Ike always said no. Finally, General Marshall changed his request to a direct order.

As 1943 ended, the forces Ike commanded had conquered Morocco, Algeria, Tunisia, Sicily, and southern Italy. Yet, the war was a long way from ending. Germany still had firm control of France and other European countries. The territory the Allies had gained had not loosened the Nazi's grip on Europe.

On January 2, 1944, Ike and Mamie were finally reunited. She saw how the war had aged Ike. She was also concerned to see that he was smoking up to four packs of cigarettes a day. But Mamie had never seen her husband so confident and self-assured. They talked of many things.

General Marshall had arranged for Ike and Mamie to

Allied leaders Premier Joseph Stalin of the U.S.S.R. and President Franklin Roosevelt of the United States met in 1943. *(Courtesy of the Library of Congress.)*

enjoy two days of complete privacy. He had his private rail car take them to a secluded cottage in Maryland. It would be their only time alone during World War II.

The rest of Ike's furlough was a working vacation. He met with President Roosevelt, General Marshall, and other military leaders to discuss the strategy and planning of "Overlord," the code name for the invasion of France. Since they fully expected to win the war, they also discussed postwar plans. The occupation and governing of Germany was a major topic.

Ike's furlough ended on January 13. Mamie was

disappointed over how little time they had spent together. She felt slighted because of her husband's complete devotion to Overlord. The prospect of another lengthy separation was almost unbearable. As she watched him pack, she told him, "Don't come back again till it's over, Ike. I can't stand losing you again."

After returning to London, Ike spent practically every waking moment planning and preparing for the great invasion. Publicly, Ike exuded great confidence in the undertaking. Privately, he worried about everything that could go wrong. The difficult task of driving out a battle-hardened, heavily armed enemy was an intimidating enterprise.

Overlord would be a direct frontal assault against a deeply entrenched enemy. The German fortifications along the coast of France were called the Atlantic Wall. The Wall formed a continuous barricade that the Allies could not outflank. The key to victory would be control of the air and sea. The Allies hoped to weaken the enemy's resistance by continuous shelling from warships and bombers.

The massive invasion known as D-Day was originally planned for June 5, 1944. On the eve of the invasion, the Allies were poised and prepared with stockpiles of military equipment, supplies, and munitions totaling nearly six million tons. They were prepared for everything—except the weather.

On the morning of June 4, Ike was informed that overcast skies would keep the Allied air forces from

General Eisenhower gives orders to paratroopers in England on June 6, 1944. *(Courtesy of the Library of Congress.)*

participating. Ike told the other Allied military leaders that air support was essential. The ground forces alone were not enough to overwhelm the enemy. They agreed to postpone the invasion for twenty-four hours.

The first wave of the massive onslaught hit the beaches of Normandy at 6:30 A.M. on June 6, 1944. Even though there had been months of planning and preparation, there were setbacks. Many soldiers became seasick while crossing the choppy waters of the English Channel. Others died needlessly when they left their landing craft too soon and drowned in deep water. Allied air bombing meant to take out German defense guns was off target.

The Allies met their strongest resistance at Omaha Beach. The bombs had landed too far inland to do the Allies much good. The fighting was fierce, furious, and bloody. Eventually, German resistance weakened under the unrelenting pressure of 4,000 ships, 11,000 planes, and thousands upon thousands of ground soldiers rolling onto the beach. By nightfall, almost 155,000 Allied troops had landed and seized about eighty square miles of occupied France.

While the beaches were being stormed, Allied planes were flying behind the Atlantic Wall and dropping tons of bombs on bridges, roads, and railroads. This constant bombardment prevented the Germans from sending reinforcements and cut off their supply routes.

After establishing beachheads, the Allies moved forward. By the end of June, over a million Allied soldiers had landed in France. Still, German resistance was strong and progress was slow. Hitler's stubborn refusal to surrender started taking its toll when 100,000 German soldiers were surrounded and captured near Falaise, France. By late August, Paris was liberated and by mid-September, Hitler's troops had withdrawn to the border of France and Germany.

On December 16, 1944, Ike received news that Congress had created a new rank of General of the Army. The prestigious rank would become better known as five-star general. Along with Ike, George C. Marshall, Douglas MacArthur, and Henry "Hap" Arnold received the esteemed designation.

Ike had no time to celebrate his promotion. The same day he heard about receiving the fifth star, the Germans launched their last great counter-offensive. At the Ardennes Forest in Belgium, the Allied troops had forged beyond the line, creating a bulge. This left a vulnerable place for attack that could separate the Allied line. In a seesaw, thirty-day Battle of the Bulge, both Allied and German troops were captured, liberated, and then re-captured. After a month of fighting, the Germans were forced to retreat.

Ike took the blame for the near-defeat. He had failed to anticipate how desperate Hitler had become. Eventually, the Allies turned the battle to their advantage. British troops on the north and American soldiers on the south combined to squeeze out the Germans. In the process, hundreds of German tanks and armored vehicles were destroyed. German casualties were estimated at over 120,000 dead, wounded, or captured. Their retreat would set the stage for the conquest of Germany.

The Germans continued to fight savagely as they retreated. Approaching the Rhine River, they held their ground instead of retreating across the river. It was a costly decision. They lost over 250,000 prisoners and an unknown number of men were killed or wounded. By this time, Germany had virtually no air force left. Allied planes were systematically bombing German cities and selected targets almost at will.

On March 7, 1945, the Allies made a major break-through. The Germans had planned to blow up a rail-road bridge in the town of Remagen, Germany. The bridge was a gateway to crossing the Rhine. A German prisoner of war warned his captors of the bridge's imminent destruction. The Allies seized the bridge and thwarted its destruction. Hitler's last natural defense was breached.

On April 23, 1945, the eastward advancing U.S. Army met the westward advancing Russian Army at the Torgau area on the Elbe River. One week later, Adolf Hitler killed himself. Two days later, Berlin fell to the Russian Army.

The formal surrender of Germany took place at a schoolhouse in Rheims, France, on May 7, 1945. Ike did not attend. He sent representatives from England, France, Russia, and the United States to accept the unconditional surrender of the German forces to the Western Allies and the Soviet Union. The ceremony was repeated in Berlin the next day, so May 8,1945 became recognized as V-E (Victory in Europe) Day.

On September 2, 1945, Japan formally surrendered after the cities of Hiroshima and Nagasaki were leveled by atomic bombs. World War II was finally over.

A message to Ike from General Marshall summed up Ike's wartime accomplishments: "You have completed your mission with the greatest victory in the history of warfare. You have commanded with outstanding success the most powerful military force that has ever been assembled . . . You have made history, great history for the good of mankind and you have stood for all we hope and admire in an officer of the United States Army."

A further testament to Ike's military and coalition building skills was given by Montgomery in his *Memoirs*:

> Allied cooperation in Europe during the Second World War was brought to the greatest heights it has ever attained. Although it may be true to say that no one man could have been responsible for such an achievement, the major share of the credit goes to Eisenhower, without any doubt . . . he was a great Supreme Commander, a military statesman. I know of no other person who could have welded the Allied forces into such a fine fighting machine in the way he did, and keep a balance among the many conflicting and disturbing elements which threatened at times to wreck the ship.

Chapter Five

Reluctant Politician

At the end of World War II, Ike was probably the world's most popular American. He was a living symbol of the triumph of America and its allies over the Nazi war machine. Inevitably, both Democrats and Republicans wanted him to lead their party to victory in the 1948 presidential election.

One month before Japan surrendered, President Harry Truman told Ike, "General there is nothing that you may want that I won't try to help you get. That definitely and specifically includes the presidency in 1948."

What Ike wanted was to simply step out of the spotlight. At age fifty-five, he thought about retiring. A leisurely life of hunting, fishing, golfing, and writing had a strong appeal. An occasional speech or lecture would bring in enough money to supplement his military pension. He claimed to have no political ambitions.

"In the strongest language you can command you can state that I have no political ambitions at all," he told reporters.

If politics was out of the question so was an early retirement. America still needed Ike. After Germany's surrender he served as military commander of the American sector of occupied Germany. In December of 1945, he succeeded General Marshall as chief of staff of the U.S. Army. As chief of staff Ike had to oversee the dismantling of America's armed forces. Disbanding an army was more difficult than commanding one.

Millions of draftees and enlisted men and women had to be discharged and transported home. There were also constant squabbles with members of Congress and the joint chiefs of staff over issues such as the size, strength, and budget of the postwar army. These conflicts taught Ike valuable lessons on how and when to compromise and when to abandon a lost cause. Ike found the job grueling. In a letter to his son, John, he called his new position, "a sorry place to light after having commanded a theater of war."

Ike also had to cope with constant requests for speeches. During his first year as chief of staff, he made forty-six major speeches to various national organizations. It seemed as if his countrymen could not get enough of their favorite general. The more he made, the more requests he received for speeches.

Ike's speaking engagements and travels brought him into contact with many of America's richest and most powerful people. Almost all of them were easily charmed and awed by his reputation as a war hero. Presidents and chief executive officers (CEOs) became Ike and Mamie's new friends. When Ike finally entered politics, they would become some of his staunchest supporters.

For the first time in years, Ike and Mamie were able to spend time together. While serving as chief of staff, Ike visited every state, and Mamie usually accompanied him. They were also able to visit Hawaii, Guam, Asia, South America, and Europe. They put the strain on their marriage from wartime separation behind them.

When Ike became chief of staff, President Truman assured him that he would only have to serve for two years. His two years would be over in December of 1947. He started weighing the many job offers he was receiving.

Major corporations were offering Ike high-level positions with corresponding salaries. He told his father-in-law that they were offering "fantastic sums," but he refused to accept a position where he felt he was being exploited or his name was being used for publicity purposes. He thought the ideal job for him would be the presidency of a small college. He could do that for a few years before retiring.

Ike did accept a college presidency, but it was at a major university instead of a small college. He became president of Columbia University in New York City. The job had first been offered to him in 1946, but he declined because he was·committed to serving as chief of staff until 1947. He suggested that his brother Milton, who was president of Kansas State College, would be a better choice.

Despite the initial rejection, Columbia University officials kept pursuing him. On June 23, 1947, Ike wrote to Columbia saying that if they made him a formal offer, he would accept it. Tom Watson, who was serving on the university's search committee, negotiated the agreement with him. As president Ike demanded that he would be free of fundraising responsibilities, excessive entertaining, and burdensome administrative details.

Columbia wanted Ike so badly they agreed to all of those conditions. They hired him in June of 1948 at a salary of $25,000 a year.

All through 1946 and 1947, book publishers had been asking Ike to write his memoirs. When he was offered a lump sum payment of $635,000, he signed a deal with Doubleday Publishers. Immediately after leaving his position as chief of staff, Ike began writing.

After gathering his wartime diaries, letters, and other documents, Ike started dictating to a pool of three secretaries. He would start at 7 A.M. while eating breakfast. The dictation would continue through lunch and dinner and usually did not end until around 11 P.M. Working at that feverish pace, he finished the 250,000 word book in three months.

The book, entitled *Crusade in Europe*, became one of the best-selling nonfiction books of 1948. The work was highly praised and eventually translated into twenty-two foreign languages. After taxes, the book earned Ike about half-a-million dollars and boosted his emerging reputation as a global statesman.

Ike did not like being president of Columbia University. He found the committee and faculty meetings boring. The unrelenting paperwork was also terribly burdensome. After only seven months on the job, he wrote, "One of the major surprises . . . is the paper work. I thought I was leaving those mountainous white piles forever."

In a futile attempt to reduce paperwork, Ike requested that every project presented be written on one typewritten page. The faculty thought it was a ridiculous request. Some faculty members joked that Ike's lips got tired if he read more than one page.

Ike's mere presence and prestige brought in funds which benefited the university. Those funds allowed them to increase faculty salaries. Yet, many professors never accepted Ike as their leader. A majority of the university's faculty had doctoral degrees. They looked down on someone who only had a bachelor's degree from a military academy.

On June 25, 1950, North Korea invaded South Korea. President Truman quickly responded by sending the U.S. Navy and Air Force to help turn back the North Koreans. Ground troops soon followed. Because he was a five-star general, the law decreed that Ike was on active duty for life, but President Truman did not call on him.

In 1948, practically every pollster, politician, and journalist had expected New York Governor Tom Dewey to soundly defeat President Truman in the November presidential election. Truman stunned the nation by pulling off an upset victory. If he wanted, Truman could run again in 1952. But Truman had other ideas. He wanted Ike to declare himself a Democrat and run for president. Then Truman could retire knowing the presidency was secure.

During the summer of 1949, President Truman tried to convince Ike to run for the U.S. Senate as New York's Democratic nominee. He sent an emissary to see him. Ike firmly rejected the offer by saying he would not even consider it.

Shortly after the Korean conflict began, Ike traveled to Washington to confer with military leaders. He did not wait for President Truman to request his services. Ike was disappointed by his meetings. In his diary he wrote that the high command "seemed indecisive."

A week later, Ike was back in Washington, this time by invitation. He testified before a Senate committee and lunched with General Marshall and President Truman. Ike assured President Truman he supported his actions, but he thought the president's military advisors were too complacent.

In October of 1950, President Truman summoned Ike to the White House and asked him to return to active duty. In 1949, America, Canada, and ten Western European nations formed an alliance called NATO (North

Atlantic Treaty Organization). The purpose of NATO was to establish a joint military defense force in Europe. Ike was asked to serve as NATO's supreme commander.

Shortly after the end of World War II, Europe was divided into free states in the west and Soviet-controlled Communist states in the east. While the U.S. was dismantling its large wartime army, the Soviets were maintaining their fighting forces at near wartime levels. Soon, the Soviet Red Army had ten times as many troops stationed in Europe as the United States. The Soviets also reneged on pledges to hold free elections in Poland, Romania, Bulgaria, and other eastern European nations they controlled.

The Soviets attempted to expand their influence into other countries. In early 1947, Greek communist guerrillas provoked a civil war in that country. An infusion of $400 million in America economic and military aid led to the eventual defeat of the communists. If the nations of Western Europe were to remain free, they would need a unified military force to repel aggression.

Ike told President Truman he would accept the position only if he were "ordered" and not "requested" to take it. They agreed, probably because it was mutually beneficial. President Truman would have Ike out of the country without having to send him to Korea. Ike could leave Columbia and return to active duty in a high profile post that would keep him in the public eye. The new post would also put Ike in close contact with Western European heads of state. This would enhance his image and reputation as a world statesman.

Taking command of NATO was a difficult task. Nearly everything about the organization was vague. Was NATO going to be a multinational force or an alliance of independent national armies? How many American troops would be stationed in Europe?

America's NATO allies were also reluctant to let Germany rearm itself. After World War II, Germany was divided into two nations—a Communist East Germany and a free West Germany. Nations such as France, Belgium, and Holland had been liberated from the Nazis for a short time. They did not want West Germany to become a military power.

While Ike was dealing with NATO's problems, he was still beseeched to run for president, a proposition he began to seriously consider. He felt the Truman Administration was not giving his old boss, General MacArthur, its full support in the Korean War. He was also concerned about the future of the Republican Party. The Democrats had won the last five presidential elections. The front runner for the Republican presidential nomination, Senator Robert Taft of Ohio, did not look like a winning candidate. He worried about the isolationist direction of many in the Republican Party. Taft and others advocated a "Fortress America." Ike thought it was dangerous for the U.S. to disengage from the world's affairs.

Ike continued to publicly maintain that he was uninterested in politics. An old army friend, General Ed Clark, tried to organize an Eisenhower-for-President movement, but Ike called Clark and told him, "I cannot even conceive of circumstances as of this moment that could convince me I had a duty to enter politics."

In January of 1951, Ike visited the eleven European capitals of the NATO member nations. He used his prestige and powers of persuasion to lobby for increased military spending by the European NATO members. One month later, he was lobbying in Washington, D.C.

On February 1, Ike addressed an informal joint session of Congress. He assured Congress that the U.S. would not be solely responsible for defending Europe from the threat of communist domination, but the U.S. would have to make a strong commitment to NATO. The U.S. would have to provide arms and other military equipment to insure NATO's success. If the U.S. did that, their European allies would respond with a firm commitment to rearm themselves.

Two months later, Congress responded by approving the movement of four divisions of soldiers, along with naval and air support to Western Europe. By the middle of 1951, NATO was shaping up as a genuine military force.

Without Ike's support, the Eisenhower-for-President movement continued to grow. Ike Clubs were formed throughout the country. In August of 1951, Oregon Democrats filed petitions to put him on the ballot in the Democratic presidential primary. President Truman still had not announced his plans for 1952, but his low approval rating made his reelection doubtful.

Ike and President Truman met in Washington in November of 1951. Once again, Ike was told the Democratic presidential nomination was his for the asking. President Truman pledged his full support if he would accept. Ike told the president his political tendencies were with the Republicans and not the Democrats.

While Ike was remaining aloof from politics, Senator Taft was edging closer to the Republican nomination. Senator Henry Cabot Lodge of Massachusetts visited Eisenhower in Paris and urged him to let the Ike Clubs enter his name in the upcoming Republican primaries. Ike was still non-committal. He merely told Senator Lodge he would think it over.

Pressure continued to mount on Ike to enter the race. In response he cited Army Regulation 600-10: "Members of the Regular Army, while on active duty, may accept nomination for public office, provided such nomination is tendered without direct or indirect activity or solicitation on their part." Ike seemed to be saying, I cannot seek the nomination, but if you want to nominate me, I cannot stop you.

On January 6, 1952, Senator Lodge announced he was entering Ike's name on the Republican ballot in the New Hampshire primary. Senator Lodge declared Ike was a Republican and that he would accept the nomination if it were offered to him. Ike would not confirm Lodge's claim of party affiliation, but he cagily admitted he voted Republican. He still refused to come out and say he wanted or would accept the nomination.

Ike's name was entered on the ballot in New Hampshire. In their March primary Ike received fifty percent of the vote to thirty-eight percent for Senator Taft. He had won the primary without even campaigning. A week later, he received over 106,000 write-in votes in the Minnesota primary. At the end of March, President Truman formally announced that he would not run for re-election.

In early April, Ike wrote President Truman a letter requesting to be relieved of his NATO duties, effective June 1, 1952. President Truman honored his request and Ike became a full fledged candidate, but he had almost waited too long. Senator Taft had been campaigning for four years and already had the votes of several hundred delegates.

On July 7, the Republican National Convention convened in Chicago. The convention was marred by a bitter and emotional fight over the credentials of several pro-Taft delegates. The Eisenhower forces won that fight; the Taft delegates were ruled out of order. Ike was nominated on the first ballot.

Ike and his supporters then turned their attention to choosing a vice-presidential candidate. Ike's running mate had to meet several criteria—he had to be younger than Ike, an energetic campaigner, a prominent anti-Communist, and from a western state. A thirty-nine-year-old California Senator named Richard M. Nixon was all of those things. He became Ike's running mate.

In late July, the Democrats held their convention. They nominated Governor Adlai Stevenson of Illinois as their presidential candidate and Senator John Sparkman of Alabama as the vice-presidential candidate.

Both Stevenson and Ike campaigned hard. Ike delivered 228 speeches while traveling over 50,000 miles. Governor Stevenson gave 203 speeches. But the campaign is best remembered for Nixon's fight to stay on the ticket when it was revealed that some wealthy California Republicans had maintained what was called a "secret slush fund" of $18,000 to supplement Nixon's $10,000 a year senatorial salary.

Several of Ike's key advisors, scared that the scandal would doom their chances, wanted Nixon off the ticket. Nixon went on national television and delivered an emotional speech. Nixon declared that the money was used only for campaign expenses. After the speech received an overwhelmingly favorable response, Ike agreed to keep Nixon on the ticket.

Despite the controversy over the Nixon fund, the Eisenhower-Nixon ticket won easily. They won fifty-five percent of the popular vote and had over six-and-a-half million more votes than the Stevenson-Sparkman ticket. Ike and Nixon also won the electoral votes of thirty-nine states to give them a 442 to 89 vote majority in the electoral college.

The Republican's simple three word slogan, "I like

Ike," summed up the feelings of the voters. Ike's enormous popularity carried over to other Republican candidates. The Republicans gained control of both houses of Congress. For the first time in twenty-four years, the Republicans held the presidency and enjoyed majority party status in both houses of Congress. Ike's first term would begin with grand hopes and great expectations.

Chapter Six

Thirty-fourth President

Between election day and inauguration day, President Truman and President-Elect Eisenhower met once. The meeting was brief and awkward and ended after twenty minutes. It was an indication of what Ike's inauguration day would be like.

President Truman and Ike had known each other since 1945 and had enjoyed a cordial, if not friendly, relationship. But during the 1952 presidential election, Ike and Nixon had attacked the Truman Administration for being corrupt, soft on Communism, and for failing to end the Korean War. Ike had pledged to travel to Korea if he was elected, and President Truman thought Ike's pledge was a contemptible political stunt. Relations between the two men hit a new low in the final days of the campaign when President Truman reportedly said, "the General doesn't know any more about politics than a pig knows about Sunday."

It was customary, but not mandatory, for the president-elect and his wife to call on the outgoing president and first lady at the White House on inauguration day. On the morning of January 20, 1953, the Eisenhower motorcade arrived at the White House at 11:30 A.M. Ike and Mamie declined an invitation to come in the White House for a cup of coffee with the Trumans. They stayed in their car until the Trumans walked out of the White House, only leaving the car to greet them.

Little was said as Ike and the outgoing president rode together to the ceremony. According to Truman, Ike broke the uncomfortable silence by remarking, "I did not attend your Inauguration in 1948 out of consideration for you, because if I had been present, I would have drawn attention from you." Truman replied, "Ike, I didn't ask you to come—or you'd been here." Ike denied that the conversation ever occurred. Whether it is true or not, there was no doubt that partisan politics had ruined their relationship.

In December 1952, before his inauguration, Ike made good on his campaign promise to visit Korea. Americans felt reassured when they saw film footage of the world's most famous general back in uniform and surveying a battlefield. Surely the man who had run the Nazis out of Europe would find a way to end this war.

Ike's visit convinced him that the U.S. was stuck in a war that could not easily be won. Over 30,000 American soldiers had been killed with no end in sight. Ike wanted to end the war as soon as possible, but he could

Ike met with President Harry Truman (left) only once after defeating the Democrats in the presidential election of 1952. *(Courtesy of the Library of Congress.)*

not abandon the South Koreans to their Northern aggressors. A negotiated settlement was the best hope of ending the war.

As always, Ike wanted to deal from a position of strength. This time he was unable to because Congress had never formally declared war on North Korea. The war was technically called a "police action." Ike used the threat of a massive arms buildup and the possibility of using nuclear weapons to bring about an end to the fighting.

On July 27, 1953, an armistice was signed. After

nearly three years of bloodshed and spending billions of dollars, neither side gained any territory. Still, Americans felt an immense sense of relief. The war was finally over and the troops would be returning home.

During his first few months as president, Ike found some members of his own party were giving him more trouble than the Democrats. The most glaring example was Senator Joseph R. McCarthy of Wisconsin.

McCarthy first gained national attention in 1950 when he claimed to have a list of "205 known Communists" working in the U.S. State Department. McCarthy later reduced the number to fifty-seven, but in a Senate speech, he raised it again to eighty-one. After making such baseless, reckless charges, McCarthy was re-elected to the Senate in 1950.

While Truman was president, Republicans had not complained when McCarthy charged that several members of the Truman Administration were communists. Then, during the 1952 presidential campaign, McCarthy had charged that Ike's old friend and mentor, General George C. Marshall, was part of the communist conspiracy. This charge enraged Truman, who respected Marshall and considered him to be a national hero.

Surely Ike would rise to defend the man who, more than anyone else, was responsible for his success. The perfect opportunity arrived during a speech Ike was to give in Milwaukee, Wisconsin—McCarthy's home state. But at the last minute a paragraph which praised Marshall was deleted from the speech. Ike had let his

Senator Joseph McCarthy accused many government officials of communist subversion. *(Courtesy of the Library of Congress.)*

political advisors convince him that defending Marshall in Wisconsin would be too big of an insult to McCarthy. They were afraid it would anger his supporters.

Ike's failure to defend General Marshall deeply angered then-President Truman so much that he loathed Ike for his lack of political courage. He thought his inaction was indefensible. At that moment, Truman changed his mind about Ike becoming president. Eisenhower defended Marshall on four different occasions during the 1952 presidential campaign, but never in a dramatic moment that would make headlines.

Various reasons have been given for Ike's failure to stand up to McCarthy. The most common one is that Ike believed the senator would eventually self-destruct. He also wanted McCarthy's support and his influence in the Senate, where it was thought that McCarthy controlled seven or eight votes.

Ike was correct in thinking that McCarthy's own excesses would finally do him in. In 1957, he was formally censured by his fellow senators. In a 67 to 22 vote, the U.S. Senate condemned McCarthy for contempt and abuse of power. However, by then McCarthy had already ruined the lives and destroyed the careers of untold numbers of honest Americans. McCarthy did not discover or expose a single communist in the U.S. government.

On May 17, 1954, the U.S. Supreme Court issued a landmark decision striking down racial segregation in public schools. In a unanimous vote the high court ruled in *Brown v. Topeka Board of Education* that so-called "separate but equal" schools for different races were inherently unequal. But the court neglected to say *when* the schools should be desegregated. The ruling was tainted with the innocuous phrase "with all deliberate speed."

The ruling would effect eleven million children in seventeen states. Two days after the decision, Ike held a press conference. When asked about the decision, Ike was noncommittal: "The Supreme Court has spoken and I am sworn to uphold the constitutional processes in this country; and I will obey." This tepid comment of support hinted at the president's true feelings. Ike wished the Supreme Court had upheld the practice of separate but equal schools. He had several southern supporters and enjoyed taking golf vacations in Augusta, Georgia, home of the Masters tournament. He believed that separating whites and blacks was the best public policy. By refusing to publicly endorse the Brown decision, Ike made it more difficult for integration to occur.

Ike put off campaigning for the 1954 congressional elections until mid-October. He thought Truman had demeaned the presidency by making partisan political speeches. Ike also believed that the rigors of campaigning would take a toll on his health.

But after seeing public opinion polls predicting big gains by the Democrats, Ike quickly changed his mind about hitting the hustings. He was also swayed by a fear that the extreme conservatives such as Senator McCarthy and his followers would take over the party if the Republicans lost control of Congress.

From mid-October to election day, Ike traveled 10,000 miles and made about forty speeches urging citizens to vote Republican. Ike campaigned in the eastern states; Vice-President Nixon campaigned in the Midwest and western states. Ike's speeches emphasized his administration's achievements—peace in Korea, a balanced budget, and reductions in federal spending. Nixon's speeches attacked the Democrats for being soft on communism.

All their campaigning and speechmaking had little effect. Ike's popularity did not extend to the Republicans in Congress. In November, the Republicans lost two seats in the Senate and eighteen in the House, and the Republicans lost control of Congress. For the rest of Ike's term, the Republicans would be the minority party in Congress.

The losses in the 1954 elections had some party leaders wondering if Ike would seek a second term. In September of 1955, a health crisis raised more doubts about the 1956 election. On September 23, while vacationing in Colorado, Ike had enjoyed an active day. He arose at 5 A.M., cooked breakfast for himself and two guests, and did some routine office work before playing some golf. He was in bed by 10 P.M.

Around 1:30 in the morning, Ike awakened with a severe pain in his chest. He asked Mamie for some milk of magnesia, but Mamie instinctively knew it was something more serious than indigestion. She called Ike's personal physician, Dr. Howard Snyder.

Dr. Snyder arrived at Ike's bedside around 2 A.M. He administered amyl nitrate to stimulate Ike's heartbeat and gave Ike sedatives to help him sleep. Ike slept till noon, and then, Dr. Snyder had Ike admitted to Fitzsimons Army Hospital in Denver.

At the hospital under Dr. Snyder's care, Ike was placed in an oxygen tent. When news of the illness was made public, Americans became alarmed. On Monday, September 26, the stock market reported $14 billion in

Mamie Eisenhower is escorted to the hospital by her son, Major John Eisenhower after Ike suffered a heart attack. *(Courtesy of the Library of Congress.)*

losses. It was clear the nation needed reassurance that Ike was okay.

The sudden illness put Vice-President Nixon in a very difficult position. Hesitancy to assume the role of interim or acting president could make him look afraid to take control. Quickly taking over would make him look cold, calculating, and uncaring. Somehow, he was able to avoid doing either one. Nixon chaired cabinet meetings and meetings of the National Security Council (NSC). Americans were relieved to see their government functioning.

Ike's recovery was smooth, but not rapid. On October 25, he took his first walk since being hospitalized. On November 11, Ike and Mamie flew to Washington before traveling on to their Gettysburg home for rest and relaxation. By Christmas, he felt like he was fully recovered. Before the end of the year, Ike was back at work in the Oval Office conducting business as usual.

In January of 1956, Ike delivered his annual State of the Union message. He presented his legislative wish list to Congress. A top priority item on the list was the construction of an interstate highway system. Ike pointed out some compelling reasons for its construction. By 1970, the number of cars on America's highways would double. Better roads would also be safer roads. Improved means of transporting goods and services would benefit the country's economy.

Congress took time to agree on how to finance the project. After some quibbling, it was decided the project

Ike stands under hundreds of balloons shortly before the 1956 elections. *(Courtesy of the Library of Congress.)*

would be funded by increased fuel taxes and taxes on tires and vehicles. On June 29, 1956, Ike signed the bill which created today's system of interstate highways.

After making peace in Korea, Ike soon had problems with other nations. France had tried to keep its colonial possession in French Indochina (now known as Vietnam), but by 1954 the nationalist Vietnamese led by Ho Chi Minh were winning the war. When France asked for air support, Ike refused, but he continued providing aid and American military advisors. U.S. aid to the French in Vietnam had begun with the Truman Administration. After the French were defeated, the United States continued economic and military assistance to South Vietnam. Eventually the U.S. would slip into its longest war.

In 1955, the Eisenhower Administration came close to using atomic weapons in a dispute between Communist China and Nationalist China in Taiwan. On January 10, the Air Force of Communist China raided the Tachen Islands which were held by Nationalist China troops. The U.S. was obligated by treaty to come to the aid and defense of Nationalist China. Two weeks after the Tachen invasion, Ike asked Congress to pass a resolution allowing the president to use armed forces without a formal declaration of war.

The resolution passed the House by a vote of 410 to 3. It breezed through the Senate with an 83 to 3 vote. Now Ike had the authority to do whatever he wanted in China, including the use of nuclear weapons. In a March 16 press conference, Ike said nuclear weapons would be used if the U.S. went to war with Communist China.

There was also concern that the two nations would go to war over a pair of islands known as Quemoy and Matsu. The islands were much closer to Communist China than to Taiwan. Conventional thinking held that the islands were not worth defending, but Ike was determined to stand up to the Communists. The threat of nuclear weapons was enough to make Communist China back down, and war was averted.

Ike steered clear of another military involvement after Egyptian President Gamal Abdel Nasser seized control of the Suez Canal in July of 1956. The 103-mile canal that links the Mediterranean and Red Seas had been built and was operated by England and France. After Egypt seized the canal, the European nations asked Ike to intervene against Egypt. He refused, saying the dispute should be mediated by the United Nations.

At times, Ike felt pressure to use nuclear weapons. Secretary of State John Foster Dulles or the joint chief of staff argued that the U.S. should use its nuclear superiority while it lasted, but the president would recall the deaths and devastation of D-Day. Ike wanted to be the president who kept the peace, not the president who started another world war.

As Ike's first term was ending, the Korean War was over and the world was at peace. The nation's economy was sound. The U.S. was strong militarily and respected in the world. There was little question that Ike could have a second term, *if* he wanted it.

Chapter Seven

Second Term

During his first term, Ike said repeatedly that he wanted to serve only one term. He had survived a serious heart attack, and he would be sixty-six years old in 1956.

In November of 1955, Adlai Stevenson announced he would make another bid for the presidency, putting increased pressure on Ike to announce his intentions. Stevenson was a formidable opponent, and most observers thought that the president was the only Republican who could beat him. About a month after the Stevenson announcement, Republican National Committee Chairman Leonard Hall told a Washington press corps that he thought the Eisenhower-Nixon team would run for reelection. Most reporters thought that was mainly wishful thinking on Hall's part.

Although he enjoyed his party's solid backing, Ike still had doubts about seeking a second term. Ike announced he would run for reelection only after his doctors assured him that he had made a full recovery.

Two months before the Republican National Convention, Ike was hospitalized again. He underwent surgery to remove blockage of his small intestine. The operation was a success, but Ike remained bedridden for three weeks.

By August, Ike had made a complete recovery. That month, the Republicans held their national convention and unanimously nominated him for a second term. Minnesota Governor Harold Stassen led a movement to dump Vice-President Nixon from the ticket, but it quickly fizzled.

The Democrats nominated Adlai Stevenson and Senator Estes Kefauver of Tennessee as his running mate. Although they had regained control of Congress in 1954, the Democrats realized they had little chance of winning the White House. The economy was stable, the country was at peace, and Ike was a popular incumbent.

Ike campaigned confidently. He waited until mid-September before making his first campaign speech. He limited his appearances and only visited thirteen of the forty-eight states. The brunt of the campaigning and speechmaking was done by Vice-President Nixon.

The Stevenson campaign was never able to cut into Ike's lead. Ike deflected the health issue by mounting a reasonably active campaign while serving as a full-time president. Stevenson also tried to win votes by calling for an end to the above-ground testing of nuclear weapons. This tactic failed because most Americans sided with Ike. Since the Russians also had nuclear weapons, continued testing was considered essential to national security.

On November 6, 1956, Ike was overwhelmingly re-elected. The Eisenhower-Nixon ticket carried forty-one of the forty-eight states and received fifty-seven per-cent of the popular vote. Ike's margin of nine-and-a-half million votes was nearly double his 1952 margin of victory. In the electoral vote, Ike and Nixon received 457 votes to just 73 for Stevenson and Kefauver. How-ever, Ike's immense popularity was not shared by other Republican candidates. The Democrats retained con-trol of Congress by gaining one seat in the Senate and picking up an additional twenty-one seats in the House.

Ike began his second term with a seventy-nine per-cent approval rating. In less than a year, it would drop to fifty–seven percent. Two major factors in the drop were Ike's reluctance to act in a school integration contro-versy and the Soviet Union's launching of the first man-made satellite.

In September 1957, nine black students tried to en-roll at the all-white Central High School in Little Rock, Arkansas. They were turned away by a mob of angry whites who surrounded the school. The harassed blacks left the school under a police escort.

Arkansas Governor Orval Faubus then sent members of the Arkansas National Guard to Central High to prevent the blacks from enrolling. This was in direct defiance of a federal court order. Ike was forced to act.

Publicly, Ike had never spoken out against racially

segregated schools. He believed that if integration was going to happen it should be a slow, gradual process. He believed that acting slowly and cautiously would prevent violence.

After meeting with Ike, Faubus pledged he would obey the federal court order to integrate Central High and other Little Rock high schools. Yet, he made no commitment to remove the National Guard troops from the Central High campus.

On Friday, September 20, 1956, a federal judge ordered Faubus and the National Guard to stop interfering with the school integration process. Ike hoped that a crisis had been averted and that integration would proceed peaceably.

The following Monday, the nine blacks avoided another angry mob by entering the school through a side door. When the mob learned they had been tricked, they tried to break through the police barricades. Once again, the nine students left the campus with a police escort. This time, they had been in school for about three hours.

Ike was out of options. On September 24, he issued an executive order dispatching federal troops to Little Rock and putting the Arkansas National Guard under federal control. The following day, soldiers from the 101st Airborne Division dispersed the mob. This time, the students were able to attend classes all day.

By October 23, the students were able to enter the school without military protection. The last members of the 101st Airborne Division left Little Rock in November, but the National Guard stayed under federal control until the end of the school year.

Ike's handling of the situation displeased both conservatives and liberals. Supporters of civil rights felt he had acted too slowly. Conservative southern officials were unhappy because the federal government had interfered with the way they ran their public schools. Although he was slow to move, when he did Ike acted decisively. He exercised the power of the presidency to enforce a federal court order.

On October 4, 1957, the Soviet Union became the first nation to launch a man-made satellite into space. It was called *Sputnik*. Throughout the United States, there was an immediate and intense reaction to this feat. Since the end of World War II, Americans had been confident they lived in the world's most scientifically advanced country. Now they were shocked to see that the Soviets had taken the lead in the "race for space."

Ike's administration tried to downplay *Sputnik*'s importance by announcing that the satellite "did not come as any surprise." That did little to calm most Americans. There was a widespread fear that if the Soviets were more scientifically advanced, then they were also militarily superior.

Ike's next response was to determine how the Soviets had taken the lead in the race for space. He met with several of America's most distinguished scientists. They organized the President's Science Advisory Committee.

The President and First Lady meet with Prime Minister of India Jawaharal Nehru and Mrs. Indira Gandhi in December 1956. *(Courtesy of the Library of Congress.)*

The near-hysteria caused by *Sputnik* became even more pronounced when the Soviets launched *Sputnik II* on November 3, 1957. *Sputnik II* was a space capsule carrying one special passenger: a dog. The U.S. suffered even further embarrassment when it dramatically failed in its first attempt to launch a satellite.

On December 6, 1957, a *Viking* rocket carrying a three-pound satellite got about five feet off the ground before toppling over and exploding. Eight weeks later, the U.S. satellite *Explorer I* was successfully launched. Only then did most Americans feel that their country was closing the gap on the Soviets in the space race.

Ike suffered a stroke in November 1957. He was at his desk signing some papers when the pen fell from his hand. After making two or three attempts, he was unable to pick the pen up. He clung to his chair while trying to stand up. After summoning his secretary, he was unable to speak clearly. "It was impossible for me to express any coherent thought whatsoever. I began to feel truly helpless," he said.

Ike thought it was merely a dizzy spell and took a nap. After his nap, he was examined by two neurological surgeons and told that he had suffered a stroke. When he failed to appear at a state dinner that evening, the press was told the president had suffered a chill.

Ike stubbornly refused to let this latest setback slow him down. He gamely attempted to resume his normal schedule before he was fully recovered. Three days after the stroke, he attended church services with Mamie. In December, he flew to Paris to address a NATO conference where he delivered an off-the-cuff speech without pausing or floundering.

A stagnant economy added to Ike's woes. As 1957 ended, unemployment was at a sixteen-year high. Ike was hoping 1958 would be a better year.

A scandal involving Ike's chief of staff, Sherman Adams, further eroded Ike's popularity and badly hurt the Republicans in the 1958 mid-term elections. In June of 1958, a congressional subcommittee found that Adams had accepted some gifts from a New England businessman who was having some tax and regulatory

The Eisenhowers celebrate Christmas together at the White House in 1957: David, Mamie, Barbara, Mary, John, Anne, Dwight, and Susan. *(Courtesy of the Library of Congress.)*

problems with the Securities and Exchange Commission (SEC). The subcommittee accused Adams of using his influence to get the SEC to clear up the problems. Ike came to Adams's defense by saying, "I admire his abilities. I respect him because of his personal and official integrity. I need him."

The Democrats doggedly continued their investigation. When evidence of more gifts was uncovered, party support for Adams diminished. Influential Senate Republicans William Knowland of California and Barry Goldwater of Arizona said Adams should resign. Ike had Vice-President Nixon talk to Adams.

Nixon tried to appeal to Adams's feelings of party loyalty. The vice-president told Adams that staying on would probably hurt the Republicans in the 1958 elections. Adams still refused to resign. He told Nixon that only the president could decide the proper thing to do. On September 22 Adams finally decided to resign. Ike announced he would accept it with "deepest regret."

The 1958 elections confirmed the worst fears of Republican Party leaders. The Democrats picked up forty-seven seats in the House and thirteen in the Senate. They also gained control of fifteen state legislatures. *Life* magazine called the Democrats midterm gains, "One of the major political landslides of the century."

Party leaders blamed the losses on Ike. The few speeches he made during the campaign were nonpartisan. He had left the campaigning and partisan speechmaking to Vice-President Nixon. In November, he did make one partisan speech attacking the Democrats, but it had little effect.

The morning after the election, Ike held a press conference. He seemed a bit baffled when reporters asked him to analyze the election results. He said that it was hard to believe that so many voters were unhappy with his administration and leadership. "I do not see where there is anything that these people want the administration to do differently. And if I am wrong, I'd like to know what it is." Privately, Ike told his closest friends that 1958 had been the worst year of his life.

Although the Democrats maintained control of Congress, Ike worked hard at easing tensions between the United States and the Soviet Union. He invited Soviet Premier Nikita Khrushchev to visit the United States. While no agreements were reached or treaties signed, the leaders of the world's two superpowers discussed their differences. The optimism and good feeling engendered by the Khrushchev visit abruptly ended when an American spy plane was shot down in Soviet airspace.

On the afternoon of May 1, 1959, Ike was informed that a spy plane had not returned from its scheduled flight. He had been told by the Central Intelligence Agency (CIA) that the aircraft would self-destruct. The plane, known as a U-2, had been flying spy missions over Russia since 1956.

The next morning, Ike got a report from the CIA that the U-2 pilot reported an engine flameout when the plane was about 1,300 miles inside the Soviet Union. It was assumed that the plane had crashed and burned, the pilot was dead, and that the plane had self-destructed. He was assured that the Soviets had no evidence it was a spy plane. He also believed the Soviets would overlook the incident. Ike and Khrushchev were scheduled to meet in Paris in mid-May. Khrushchev would probably comment privately at their Paris summit conference and avoid making a public issue.

Those hopes were shattered on May 5, when Khrushchev made a long, angry speech denouncing the U.S. for undermining the upcoming summit conference by spying. Ike still believed the Soviets had no evidence. He assumed the pilot was dead and the aircraft was in ruins. He decided to try a cover-up.

On the afternoon of May 5, Ike issued a statement saying the U-2 was a weather plane which had veered off course. The hastily arranged cover-up unraveled two days later when Khrushchev gleefully announced: "We have parts of the plane and we have the pilot who is alive and kicking."

Ike was caught in a lie, but instead of admitting it, he made things worse by telling another lie. He had the U.S. State Department issue a statement denying that the U-2 had been authorized to fly over the Soviet Union.

After Krushchev announced the U-2 pilot, Francis Gary Powers, would be put on trial, Ike held a press conference. In a prepared statement he called spying "a distasteful but vital necessity." He refused to apologize to Krushchev and insisted that his outlook for a successful summit conference had not changed.

Ike's outlook was unchanged, but Krushchev was determined to use the U-2 incident to his advantage. At the summit conference in Paris, Ike informed Krushchev that he had ended the U-2 flights and he hoped the summit conference could move on to other matters. The Soviet leader still insisted on an apology. When he did not get it, he withdrew the Soviet delegation from the conference.

Ike's second administration suffered one final disappointment when the Republicans lost control of the White House in 1960. Ike remained neutral until Vice-President Nixon was officially nominated as the Republican Party's presidential candidate at the party's convention in July. To oppose Nixon, the Democrats nominated Massachusetts Senator John F. Kennedy. Handsome, articulate, and photogenic, Kennedy was only forty-three years old. He would become the youngest man ever elected president of the United States.

Ike disliked both Kennedy and his running mate, Texas Senator Lyndon B. Johnson. Ike described Kennedy as a "young whippersnapper" He also said of Johnson: "He is a small man. He hasn't got the depth of mind nor the breadth of vision to carry great responsibility."

Nixon hoped that Ike would emphasize the important role and duties he had performed as vice-president. He waited for the president to describe him using words such as "indispensable" or "invaluable." That hope was destroyed when Ike made an unfortunate comment. When journalists pressed Ike to name one major idea Nixon had contributed during his eight years as vice-president, he replied: "If you give me a week, I might think of one. I don't remember." Ike was quick to apologize to Nixon, but the damage had already been done. The speeches Ike later made for the Nixon campaign did little to make voters forget that damaging remark.

On November 8, 1960, John F. Kennedy was elected in one of the closest presidential elections in American history. Of the sixty-eight million votes cast, Kennedy's margin over Nixon was only 118,000 votes.

However, presidential elections are decided by receiving a majority of the votes in the electoral college. The number of each state's electoral votes is equal to the number of its congressional representatives (Senators plus Congressmen). Nixon won the electoral votes of twenty-six states, but Kennedy won more of the heavily populated states. That gave him an electoral vote majority of 303 to Nixon's 219.

Ike was deeply disappointed by the outcome. He considered it a repudiation of his eight years as president. Ike told his friend "Slats" Slater, "Well, this is the biggest defeat of my life."

In the ten weeks between the election and inauguration day, Ike prepared himself for retirement. He met with President-Elect Kennedy and briefed him on the problems and responsibilities he would inherit and assume. On January 17, 1961, three days before Kennedy's inauguration, Ike went on nationwide radio and television to give his last speech as president. The soldier and president who had fought for freedom and worked for peace gave an unexpected warning about the growing influence of the military establishment and the weapons industry: "In the councils of government, we must guard against the acquisition of unwarranted influence, whether sought or unsought, by the military-industrial complex. The potential for the disastrous rise of misplaced power exists and will persist."

Satisfied that he had shared his innermost thoughts and misgivings with his countrymen, Ike left Washington for his Gettysburg, Pennsylvania, farm.

Chapter Eight

A Sense of Duty

On the morning of January 21, 1961, Ike awoke and, for the first time in nearly fifty years, his time was truly his own. No classes, no duty posts, no conferences, no appointments, no speeches to give, and no reports to read or memos to write.

After a half-century of achievement and accomplishment, Ike was not going to loaf the rest of his life away. As long as his health allowed, he enjoyed an active and productive retirement. He painted, wrote books, played golf and bridge, traveled, entertained friends, and served as one of the Republican's elder statesmen. He also found time to fish, hunt, and to tend his farm.

Ike had only been retired about three months before President Kennedy called to request a consultation. In April 1961, an army of Cuban exiles invaded their homeland and attempted to oust Cuban dictator, Fidel Castro. The 1,500-man army had been trained, armed, and financed by the U.S. Central Intelligence Agency (CIA).

The army was led to believe that U.S. military forces would come to their aid if Castro's forces overwhelmed them. But after three days of fighting, the promised aid had never arrived and the invaders surrendered. The invasion, which became known as the Bay of Pigs, had been planned and approved during the Eisenhower Administration, but it was carried out by President Kennedy.

In the aftermath of the ill-fated invasion, Ike met with President Kennedy at Camp David, Maryland. Shortly into their meeting, President Kennedy admitted the invasion was a complete failure. Ike listened politely and respectfully, but he did not shy away from asking some tough questions. He asked President Kennedy if he had met with the National Security Council (NSC) and discussed the pros and cons before launching the invasion.

The answer was no. Ike also asked why air cover had not been provided. Kennedy told Ike he wanted to try to conceal the extent of U.S. involvement in the invasion. President Kennedy said he had been hampered by worries about a response from the Soviet Union.

Ike believed that one should deal with one's enemies from a position of strength. "The Soviets follow their own plans," Ike told the president, "and if they see us show any weakness that is when they press us the hardest." Despite their disagreements, Ike told President Kennedy he would still support anything which would keep communism out of the Western Hemisphere.

On October 14, 1963, Ike celebrated his seventy-third birthday. Considering that he had suffered a heart attack, a stroke, and had major surgery for ileitis, he still engaged in a lot of physical activities. Golf, gardening, and farm chores kept him active. Following national and world events and writing his memoirs kept his mind engaged.

The first volume of his memoirs, *Mandate for Change 1953-1956*, was published in 1963 and dedicated to Mamie. The second volume, *Waging Peace 1956-1961*, was published in 1965. The two volumes totaled over 1,400 pages and gave a comprehensive account of the Eisenhower Administration from Ike's perspective.

Although the memoirs were detailed, factual, and accurate, they did not receive critical acclaim. The third book Ike wrote during his retirement was much better received. *At Ease: Stories I Tell to Friends* was published in 1967 and reprinted in several foreign language editions. In *At Ease*, Ike reminisced about his childhood, adolescence, and four years at West Point. His breezy, anecdotal writing style made it a popular book.

Along with books, Ike penned articles for popular magazines such as *Reader's Digest* and the *Saturday Evening Post*. He was also a prolific letter writer. During his retirement, he received around 7,500 letters every month and claimed to respond to two-thirds of them.

On November 22, 1963, President Kennedy was assassinated while riding in a motorcade in Dallas, Texas. Ike was attending a luncheon at the United Nations in

New York City when he received the news. The next day, he traveled to Washington to view the flag-draped casket and pay his respects to the president's widow, Jacqueline.

While in Washington, Ike honored a request to meet with the new President Lyndon B. Johnson. President Johnson asked Ike for support and told him he would regularly ask for his advice and counsel. Ike agreed to support Johnson on matters they agreed on, such as U.S. involvement in the Vietnam War, although he thought Johnson's domestic programs were too costly.

During the 1964 presidential primaries, Arizona Senator Barry Goldwater emerged as the leading candidate for the Republican nomination. Ike refused to endorse any candidate, but it was well known that he would rather see the nomination go to someone less conservative. Henry Cabot Lodge and Governor William Scranton of Pennsylvania were two of his preferences. At different times, he encouraged both politicians to oppose Senator Goldwater.

In mid-July of 1964, the Republicans held their convention in San Francisco. Even though he was working as a television commentator for ABC News, Ike addressed the convention. When he gave his speech, it was a foregone conclusion that Senator Goldwater would be the nominee. Ike's speech was a plea for party unity between the Goldwater supporters and the faction which backed Governor Scranton.

During his address, Ike was interrupted forty times

by applause from the delegates. But it was one particular remark that got the strongest reaction from his audience. Ike urged the delegates to not let themselves be divided by "those outside our family, including sensation seeking columnists and commentators . . . who couldn't care less about the good of our party." That statement set off a deafening roar of boos directed toward the press section by delegates who stood on their chairs, shouting, cursing, and shaking their fists at the reporters.

After Goldwater was nominated, Ike gave the Arizona senator his tepid support. He refused to sign a statement of support unless forty or fifty prominent party leaders signed it first. He begged off making any speeches, but he did agree to endorse Goldwater on television. They appeared together in a videotaped show. Ike called charges that Goldwater was a warmonger "tommyrot."

Unlike the tight Nixon-Kennedy race, the 1964 election was a landslide victory for Democrats. President Johnson received sixty-one percent of the popular vote and he carried forty-four of fifty states. The Democrats also won overwhelming majorities in both houses of Congress. In the Senate, they added a seat to give them a 68 to 32 edge. In the House, they picked up an additional thirty-seven seats.

Prior to the election, President Johnson had been increasing America's involvement in the Vietnam War. By the end of 1965, the U.S. had 180,000 troops in

Vietnam. One year later, it had increased to 400,000. More troops also meant more casualties. Support for the war was waning. President Johnson sought Ike's support for an increasingly unpopular war. He hoped it would help to stem the tide of anti-war public opinion.

Johnson asked for advice. He had a genuine respect for Ike's knowledge of military matters. During the Vietnam War, Americans who wanted to escalate the war effort were called hawks. Those who opposed escalation and preferred to end U.S. involvement were known as doves. Ike was definitely a hawk. He opposed negotiating a peace treaty until the U.S. had the upper hand. As always, he believed that one only negotiates from a position of strength. He even encouraged the bombing of North Vietnam. The possibility that those attacks would drag China or the Soviet Union into the war did not worry him. At a meeting with President Johnson in February 1965, Ike said, "if they threaten to intervene we should pass the word back to them to take care lest dire results occur to them."

Ike remained steadfast in his support of the war, but Johnson began to waver as casualties mounted and antiwar protests raged across the country. In February of 1968, Minnesota Senator Eugene McCarthy defeated President Johnson in the New Hampshire primary. McCarthy ran as an anti-war candidate. A president who had won a landslide victory in 1964 was now wondering if his party would re-nominate him in 1968.

In March of 1968, President Johnson went on national television and announced he was dropping out of the presidential race. Ike was outraged that he would be quitting in the midst of a war. From then on, Ike had nothing else to do with President Johnson and his administration.

With President Johnson out of the race, Senator McCarthy, New York Senator Robert F. Kennedy and Vice-President Hubert Humphrey all began vying for the Democratic presidential nomination. After Senator Kennedy was assassinated in June of 1968, Humphrey became the front runner for the nomination. In August he became the Democrat's nominee. Senator Edwin Muskie of Maine was nominated as the vice-presidential candidate.

The Republicans also had several candidates competing for their party's presidential nomination. Former Vice-President Nixon emerged as an early favorite even though he had not held elective office since 1961. Other contenders for Republican nomination were Michigan Governor George Romney, New York Governor Nelson Rockefeller, and California Governor Ronald Reagan.

Ike had a long-standing policy of not endorsing a candidate before the party held its national convention. He ended that practice by endorsing his former vice-president on July 17, 1968. Ike issued a statement saying he supported Nixon "because of my admiration of his personal qualities: his intellect, acuity, decisiveness, warmth, and above all, his integrity."

When he released the statement, Ike was bedridden at Walter Reed Hospital in Washington, D.C. He had suffered his third major heart attack in April at age seventy-seven.

The Republican National Convention convened in Miami on August 5, 1968. That night, Ike exchanged his hospital gown for a suit and tie. Television cameras were brought into his hospital room, and he addressed the assembled delegates. It was his final political speech. The next morning, he suffered another heart attack.

The latest heart attack caused Ike's heart to fibrillate. The heart would vibrate instead of beat, so no blood was pumping through it. Electrical impulses were used to restore a regular heartbeat. His son, John, began making funeral preparations, but Ike's heart improved. A few days later, Ike was receiving visitors again.

On November 5, 1968, Richard M. Nixon narrowly defeated Vice-President Humphrey. Nixon's popular vote margin was just over 510,000. Since Alabama Governor George Wallace ran as a third party candidate, Nixon received less than fifty percent of the popular vote. Governor Wallace received almost ten million votes. Nixon fared better in the electoral college vote. He carried thirty-two states and won 301 electoral votes to Humphrey's 191 and Wallace's 46. The race was much closer than Ike liked, but he was elated that Nixon had won.

In December the Eisenhower and Nixon families were united by the marriage of Ike's grandson David and

President-Elect Nixon's daughter Julie. Ike was too ill to attend, but he watched the wedding on closed circuit television.

In February of 1969, Ike's suffered yet another set-back. Scar tissue which had formed from his 1957 ile-itis operation had wrapped itself around his intestine, causing a blockage. Ike had to undergo a major ab-dominal operation. The doctors were concerned that Ike's heart could not survive the surgery, but it did—for a while.

On Monday, March 24, 1969, Ike's frail condition steadily worsened. Tubes were inserted into his nostrils so he could receive oxygen. Ike knew the end was near. He gave his son, John, some final instructions: "Be good to Mamie."

Ike died on Friday, March 28, 1969, at 12:25 P.M. His last words were, "I've always loved my wife. I've always loved my children. I've always loved my grandchildren. And I have always loved my country."

Upon learning of Ike's death, President Nixon issued a proclamation making Monday, March 31, a national day of mourning. He also ordered flags at all federal buildings, American embassies, and military installa-tions to be flown at half-staff for the next thirty days.

On Sunday, March 30, a funeral procession moved Ike's closed coffin from Washington Cathedral to the Capitol. The solemn procession included 185 chiefs of state, heads of government, and other dignitaries from seventy-five nations. In the rotunda of the Capitol,

President Nixon stood before Ike's coffin and paid tribute to his political benefactor. He praised Ike as "one of the giants of our time" and noted that he "was probably loved by more people in more parts of the world than any President America ever had. He captured the deepest feelings of free men everywhere"

On Wednesday, April 2, Ike's body was returned to Abilene. A throng estimated at 100,000 people crowded into the town to pay their final respects. President Nixon and President Johnson were among the 300 invited guests seated inside the chapel of the Eisenhower Center. After a dignified forty-five minute ceremony, Ike was buried in his army uniform in a crypt beneath the chapel floor.

With the passage of time, Ike's stature as a leader and decision-maker has increased. A 1962 poll of seventy-five historians ranked him twenty-second among the thirty-four presidents. In a 1982 survey of forty-nine historians, Ike had moved up to ninth place. Most recently, a 1994 survey by the Research Institute of Sienna College placed Ike eighth among the forty-one presidents they ranked.

The Eisenhower administration had its share of setbacks and disappointments. One major criticism is that Ike failed to exercise his moral authority as president to push for school desegregation and civil rights legislation. However, when he did act in the Little Rock crisis, he used the full force of the federal government to enforce a federal court order.

Like all presidential candidates, Ike was ambitious. Sometimes his ambition got the best of him. His failure to strongly defend General George Marshall from the attacks of Senator McCarthy, for fear it would harm his chances of becoming president, is an example of his failing to do the right thing.

Perhaps the most apt description of the Eisenhower presidency is the term "hidden hand" presidency. Until recently, the conventional view was that Ike was a detached and delegating president. He often appeared to be aloof from politics and partisanship. In his first year as president, he did not even submit a legislative program to Congress. The revised view is that Ike shrewdly wielded power behind the scenes to accomplish his goals. Like a puppeteer, he exerted control without being observed.

Even Ike's critics and detractors will admit that his eight years as president were a time of peace and prosperity. There were no wars and the economy grew for most of those years. But most importantly to Americans who lived during the 1950s, he was a man who became president because of a sense of duty, not because he lusted for political power or sought to punish enemies and reward friends. It is no wonder that so many Americans could truly say: "I like Ike."

Appendix

Eisenhower and the Interstate Highway System

Somewhere between Washington D.C., and San Francisco in the summer of 1919, Lieutenant Colonel Dwight D. Eisenhower gained his lifelong appreciation for a good road. The U.S. Army had scheduled its first transcontinental convoy that year, and Ike had eagerly signed up to go. It did not take long for him and the other soldiers to realize that cross-country travel was an arduous task. The convoy drove on slow and dangerous roads that were oftentimes covered with mud, sand, ice, or snow; weak bridges threatened to give way at any moment under the heavy trucks; and they spent long hours standing around listlessly while army mechanics repaired vehicles damaged on rutted roads.

When Ike was elected president in 1952, he vowed to modernize the nation's roads. Data from the Bureau of Public Roads showed that only twenty-four percent of the interstate roads were adequate for traffic. Inspired by how the *autobahn* had sped his troops advance into Germany during World War II, he imagined an interconnected system of multi-lane roads in the United States that would "protect the vital interest of every citizen in a safe and adequate highway system."

In 1954, Ike initiated the first phase of his plan with the passage of the Federal Highway Act, which authorized $175 million towards the interstate system. Next, Ike appealed to the nation's governors to support a partnership between federal and state governments to promote a fifty billion dollar highway program. "Together," Ike said, "the united forces of our communication and transportation systems are dynamic elements in the very name we bear—United States."

Responses to Ike's plan were mixed. The biggest debate was who would pay for the system: federal or state government. Others were angry because Ike wanted to pay for the highways through gasoline taxes. They argued that states should have control of these funds.

Representative George H. Fallon of Maryland drafted a bill for the "National System of Interstate and Defense Highways" in 1955. His bill included a highway-user tax increase to help create revenue to support the project. He proposed that ninety percent of the interstate system would be funded by federal dollars, the remaining amount to be picked up by the states. But when the bill was presented to the House on July 27, it was defeated because of controversy over funding. Not one to give up, when President Eisenhower gave his State of the Union Address on January 5, 1956, he again pledged his support for the interstate highway system.

Fallon introduced a revised bill on January 26. Although the federal-to-state revenue ratio remained the same, this time Fallon included that funding would be provided on a "pay-as-you-go" basis. That is, the federal government would allocate funds based on each state's estimate for completion of the project. At the same time, Representative Hale Boggs of Louisiana introduced a bill to increase gas and highway taxes for additional revenue. The combined Fallon and Boggs bill was passed by the House in April, and although it met resistance in the Senate, it was eventually passed in June with slight adjustments.

The passage of the Federal-Aid Highway Act of 1956 formalized the nation's highway system, standardizing not only roads, but bridges and tunnels, road signs and highway numbering. It also required that roadway workers be guaranteed no less than the prevailing wage in the area that the project was being built. President Eisenhower was sick with ileitis when he received the news that the bill had passed, and he signed the Federal-Aid Highway Act of 1956 into law from his hospital bed.

In honor of Ike's determination to provide a safe and effective network of interstate highways in America, in October 1990, President George Bush honored him by renaming the interstate highway system the "Dwight D. Eisenhower System of Interstate and Defense Highways."

Timeline

1890—Dwight David Eisenhower born in Denison, Texas.

1909—Graduates from Abilene High School, Abilene, Texas.

1914—World War I begins.

1915—Graduates from the U.S. Military Academy at West Point.

1916—Marries Mamie Doud.

1926—Graduates first in a class of 275 at Command and General Staff School.

1935—Begins serving as assistant to General Douglas MacArthur.

1939—Germany invades Poland; World War II begins.

1941—Japan bombs U.S. naval base at Pearl Harbor on December 7; U.S. enters World War II.

1942—Moves to London as commander of American forces.

1943—Directs the Allied campaign in North Africa.

1944—Directs D-Day invasion of France.

1945—Serves as commander of U.S. occupation forces in Europe.

1948—Appointed president of Columbia University.
1950—Serves as commander of the NATO forces in Europe.
1952—Elected president of the United States.
1956—Reelected to second term as president.
1961—Retires to farm in Gettysburg, Pennsylvania.
1969—Dies and is buried in Abilene, Texas.

Sources

CHAPTER ONE

p. 10, "If we were poor . . ." Dwight D. Eisenhower, *At Ease: Stories I Tell to Friends* (Garden City, NY: Doubleday & Company, 1967), 36.

p.12, "You can't keep healthy boys . . ." George Johnson, *Eisenhower* (Derby, CT: Monarch Books, 1962), 14.

p. 13, "My father legislated the matter . . ." Eisenhower, *At Ease*, 51.

p. 14, "He that conquerth his own soul . . ." Ibid., 52.

p. 16, "So thoroughly did Bob . . ." Ibid., 89-90.

p. 17, "was the best amateur . . ." Ibid., 101.

p. 18, "I changed from one job . . ." Ibid., 102.

p. 19, "This was a good day . . ." Ibid., 106.

CHAPTER TWO

p. 22, "Mr. Dumbgard what is your . . ." Eisenhower, *At Ease,* 18.

p. 22, "I'm never going to crawl . . ." Ibid., 18.

p. 22, "One of the most promising backs . . ." Stephen E. Ambrose, *Eisenhower: Soldier, General of the Army, President-Elect 1890-1952* (New York: Simon & Schuster, 1983), 49.

p. 23, "Life seemed to have little meaning . . ." Eisenhower, *At Ease*, 16.

p. 26, "This girl and I like to whirl . . ." Ibid., 9.

p. 27, "Because I was a lazy student . . ." Ibid., 18.

p. 27, "the foggiest notion of how to begin . . ." Ibid., 19.

p. 29, "as big as life . . ." Piers Brendon. *Ike: His Life and Times.* (New York: Harper & Row, 1986), 37.

p. 29, "would thoroughly enjoy his army life . . ." Ambrose, *Eisenhower: Soldier*, 51.

p. 29, "was born to command . . ." Ibid., 51.

CHAPTER THREE

p. 30, "It would please me . . ." Ambrose, *Eisenhower: Soldier*, 56.

p. 31, "Sorry, I'm on guard . . ." Eisenhower, *At Ease*, 113.

p. 31, "We didn't ask you to . . ." Ibid., 113.

p. 31, "The one who attracted my eye . . ." Ibid., 113.

p. 32, "Our new Captain, Eisenhower by name . . ." Ambrose, *Eisenhower: Soldier*, 61.

p. 36, "was the greatest disappointment of my life . . ." Ibid., 75.

p. 37, "a sort of graduate school . . ." Ibid., 77.

p. 37, "the one figure to whom I owe . . ." Ibid., 77.

p. 38, "deeply grateful for the administrative . . ." Ibid., 94.

p. 38, "This is the best officer in the Army . . ." Ibid., 93.

p. 40, "He [MacArthur] apparently thinks . . ." Ibid., 106.

p. 42, "were nil . . ." Ibid., 119.

CHAPTER FOUR

p. 43, "I'm having the time of my life . . ." Ambrose, *Eisenhower: Soldier*, 120.

p. 44, "Had it been a real war . . ." Ibid., 130.

p. 54, "The performances in Africa, Sicily and Italy . . ." *New York Times*, March 29, 1969.

p. 56, "Don't come back again till it's over . . ." Ambrose, *Eisenhower: Soldier*, 280.

p. 60, "You have completed your mission . . ." Ibid., 408.

CHAPTER FIVE

p. 62, "General there is nothing that you may want . . ." Dwight D. Eisenhower, *Crusade in Europe* (Garden City, N.Y: Doubleday & Company, 1948), 444.

p. 62, "In the strongest language . . ." Brendon, *His Life*, 188.

p. 63, "a sorry place to light after . . ." Ambrose, *Eisenhower: Soldier*, 433.

p. 64, "fantastic sums" Ibid., 469.

p. 66, "One of the major surprises . . ." Ibid., 481.

p. 67, "seemed indecisive" Ibid., 494.

p. 70, ". . . I cannot even conceive of circumstances . . ." Ibid., 500.

p. 71, "Members of the Regular Army . . ." Ibid., 520.

CHAPTER SIX

p. 75, "the General doesn't know any more . . ." Stephen E.Ambrose, *Eisenhower: The President, Vol. II* (New York: Simon & Schuster, 1984), 14.

p. 76, "I did not attend your inauguration . . ." Ibid., 41.

p. 76, "Ike I didn't ask you . . ." Ibid., 42.

p. 78, "205 known Communists . . ." Thomas C. Reeves, *The Life and Times of Joe McCarthy, A Biography* (New York: Stein and Day, 1982), 224.

p. 80, "with all deliberate speed . . ." Ed Cray, *Chief Justice A Biography of Earl Warren* (New York: Simon & Schuster, 1997), p. 295.

p. 80, "The Supreme Court has spoken . . ." Ambrose, *Eisenhower: The President*, 190.

CHAPTER SEVEN

p. 92, "did not come as any surprise . . ." Brendon, *His Life*, 348.

p. 94, "It was impossible for me to express . . ." Dwight D. Eisenhower, *Waging Peace* (Garden City, N.Y: Doubleday & Company, 1965), 227.

p. 95, "I admire his abilities . . ." Ambrose, *Eisenhower: The President*, 468.

p. 96, "deepest regret . . ." Ibid., 482.

p. 96, "I do not see where there is anything . . ." *Time*, November 17, 1958, 19.

p. 98, "We have parts of the plane . . ." Ibid., 574.

p. 98, "a distasteful but vital necessity . . ." Ibid., 576.

p. 99, "young whippersnapper . . ." Brendon, *His Life*, 397.

p. 99, "He is a small man. He hasn't got . . ." Ambrose,
　　Eisenhower: The President, 596-597.
p. 99, "If you give me one week . . ." Ibid., 600.
p. 100, "Well, this is the biggest defeat . . ." Ibid., 604.
p. 100, "In the councils of government . . ." Ibid., 612.

CHAPTER EIGHT

p. 103, "The Soviets follow their own plans . . ." Ambrose,
　　Eisenhower: The President, 638.
p. 106, "those outside our family, including . . ." *New York
　　Times,* July 15, 1964, 1.
p. 107, "if they threaten to intervene . . ." Ambrose, *Eisenhower:
　　The Preisdent,* 657.
p. 108, "because of my admiration . . ." Ibid., 672.
p. 110, "Be good to Mamie . . ." Ibid., 674.
p. 110, "I've always loved my wife . . ." *New York Times,*
　　March 31, 1969, 1.
p. 110, "one of giants of our time . . ." Ibid.

Bibliography

BOOKS

Ambrose, Stephen E. *Eisenhower: The President, Vol. II.* New
York: Simon and Schuster, 1984.

———. *Eisenhower: Soldier and President.* New York:
Touchstone, 1990.

———. *Eisenhower: Soldier, General of the Army, President-
Elect.* New York: Simon and Schuster, 1983.

Barron, Rachel. *Richard Nixon: American Politician.*
Greensboro, NC: Morgan Reynolds Inc., 1999.

Brendon, Piers. *Ike: His Life and Times.* New York: Harper
and Row, 1986.

Brodie, Fawn. *Richard Nixon: The Shaping of His Character.*
New York: W.W. Norton & Company, 1981.

Cray, Ed. *Chief Justice: A Biography of Earl Warren.* New
York: Simon & Schuster, 1997.

Degregorio, William A. *The Complete Book of U.S. Presidents.* New York: Barricade Books, 1993.

Eisenhower, Dwight D. *At Ease: Stories I Tell to Friends.* Garden City, N.Y.: Doubleday, 1967.
───. *Crusade in Europe.* Garden City, NY: Doubleday, 1948.
───. *Mandate for Change.* Garden City, NY: Doubleday, 1963.
───. *Waging Peace.* Garden City, NY: Doubleday, 1965.

Ellis, Rafaela. *Dwight D. Eisenhower: Thirty-fourth President of the United States.* Ada, OK.: Garrett Educational Corporation, 1989.

Faber, Doris. *Dwight Eisenhower.* New York: Abelard-Schuman, 1977.

Ferrara, Peter L. *NATO: An Entangled Alliance.* New York: Franklin Watts, 1984.

Johnson, George. *Eisenhower.* Derby, CT: Monarch Books, 1962.

Lyon, Peter. *Eisenhower: Portrait of the Hero.* Boston: Little, Brown and Company, 1974.

McCullough, David. *Truman*. New York: Simon & Schuster, 1992.

Montgomery, General Bernard L. *The Memoirs of Field-Marshal Montgomery*. Cleveland: World Publishing Company, 1958.

Reeves, Thomas C. *The Life and Times of Joe McCarthy, A Biography*, New York, Stein and Day, 1982.

Sulzberger, C.L. *The American Heritage Picture History of World War II*. The American Heritage Publishing Co. Inc., 1966.

PERIODICALS
"The G.O.P Wasn't Pushed—It Jumped." *Life*. November 17, 1958, 36G.

New York Times. March 28, 1969. March 29, 1969.March 30, 1969. March 31, 1969.April 2, 1969.April 3, 1969.

Time. November 17, 1958.

Index